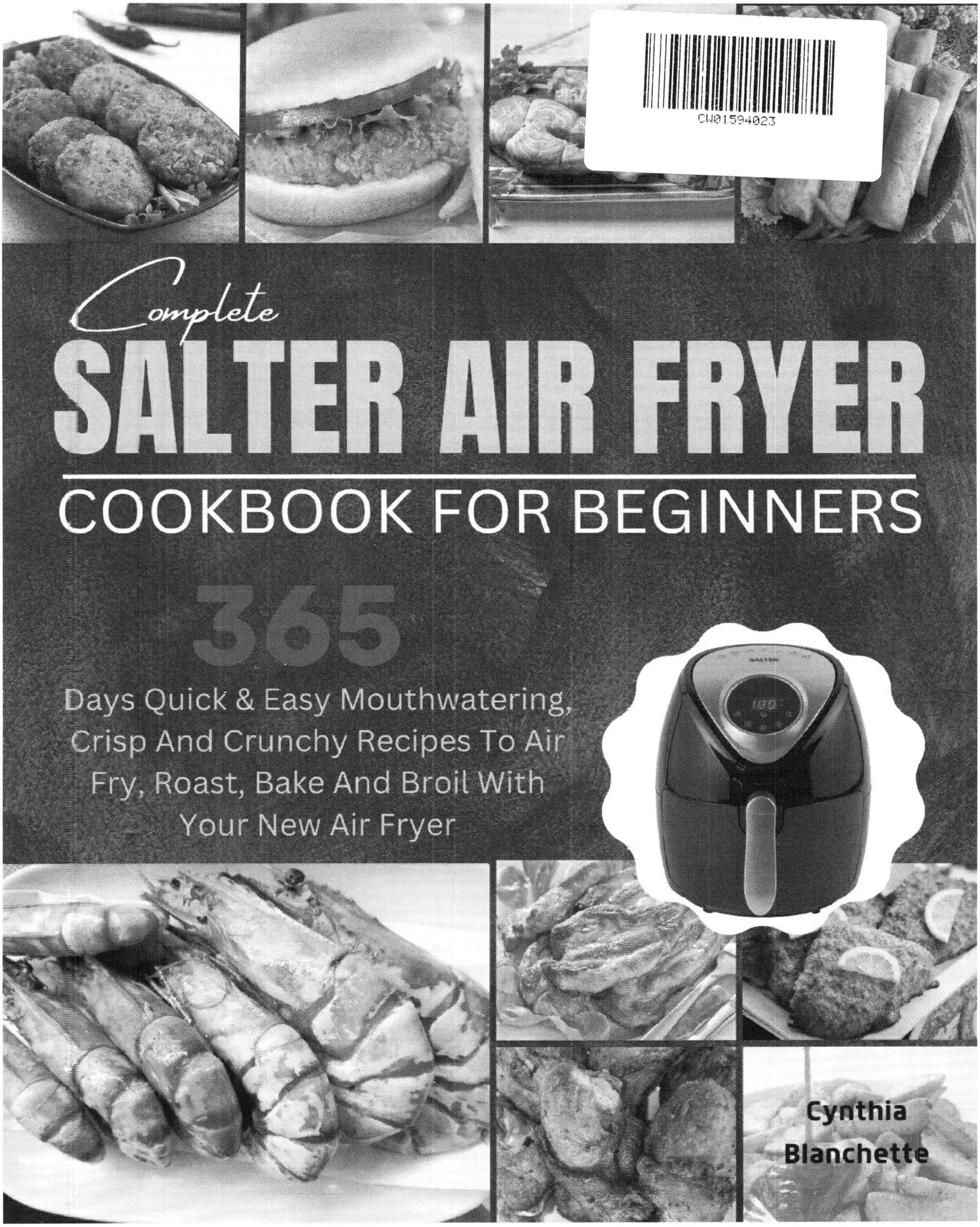
Complete
SALTER AIR FRYER
COOKBOOK FOR BEGINNERS
365
Days Quick & Easy Mouthwatering, Crisp And Crunchy Recipes To Air Fry, Roast, Bake And Broil With Your New Air Fryer
SALTER
Cynthia
Blanchette

Complete SALTER AIR FRYER

365

Days Quick & Easy Mouthwatering, Crisp And Crunchy Recipes To Air Fry, Roast, Bake And Broil With Your New Air Fryer

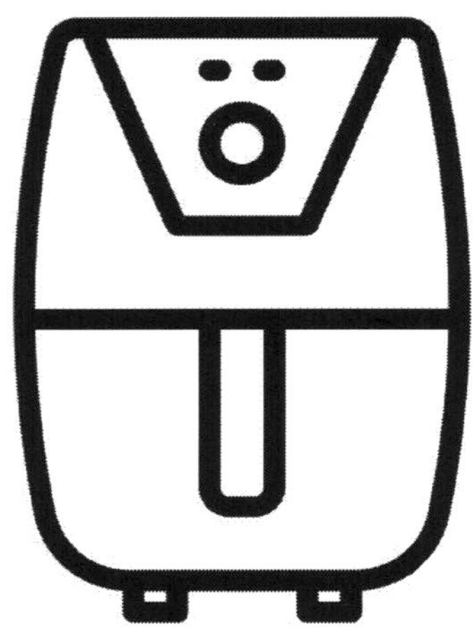

Cynthia Blanchette

CONTENTS

INTRODUCTION

The Salter Air fryer is a convenient appliance that makes it simple to cook delicious food that is also good for you. The machine uses rapid circulation of hot air to cook food, which is preferable to the more traditional method of frying food in oil and heated fat, which can be hazardous to one's health. This makes it possible for the exterior of your dish to get crisp and ensures that the layers on the inside are cooked through completely.

We are able to cook an extremely diverse range of foods and dishes because to the versatility of our Salter Air fryer. The Salter Air fryer gives you the flexibility to cook a wide variety of foods, including meat, vegetables, poultry, fruit, fish, and even a few sweets. You are able to plan every aspect of your meal, from the appetizers to the desserts and everything in between. In addition, the Salter Air fryer makes it possible to prepare handmade preserves in addition to scrumptious pies and cakes.

Functions of the Salter Air fryer

The Salter Air fryer makes use of rather straightforward technologies in its operation. The crisp texture of fried foods is caused by the rapid and even heating of the surface of the food by the hot oil used in the frying process. Because it is such a good heat conductor, oil enables all of the components to be cooked at the same time and in a shorter amount of time. For decades, people have been using convection ovens to imitate frying and to ensure that the entire surface of the meal is cooked. However, the air never circulates quickly enough to reach the appropriate level of crispiness on the surface of fried foods. In order to "air fry" things like fish, poultry, chips, and other similar items, this system circulates air at high temperatures, reaching up to 200 degrees Celsius. In comparison to the conventional method of deep frying, this method cuts the amount of fat content in food by as much as 80 percent, which has fundamentally changed the way people think about cooking.

The Salter Air fryer prepares food in a manner that is better for you and more socially acceptable by utilizing a heating element. Additionally, there is an exhaust fan just above the cooking chamber that supplies the required ventilation for the dish to be cooked properly. Food is cooked in this manner using a constant heat source from the air. This ensures that each individual item of food is subjected to the same level of heat during the cooking process. With nothing more than a grill and an exhaust fan, the Salter Air fryer is able to boost airflow at a consistent and rapid rate, making it possible to prepare healthful meals with far less fat.

The temperature rises as a result of an increase in the internal pressure, which is then managed by the exhaust system. In addition, the exhaust fan delivers additional air that has been filtered, allowing the food to be cooked in a significantly more wholesome manner. The odorless and risk-free nature of the Salter Air fryer contributes to its high level of user and environmental friendliness.

Salter Air Fryer Benefits

- Provides more cooking alternatives.
- A method of cooking that is less dangerous than deep-frying in oil that is left uncovered.
- Meals that are healthier and do not contain oil

- The scents of cooking are eliminated by air filters contained within the device.
- Reduces the amount of time spent cleaning as a result of the lack of oil and grease
- The Salter Air Fryer has the ability to bake, grill, roast, and fry, which offers a variety of cooking options. It comes equipped with a digital timer in addition to the standard options of being able to set and leave.

The Salter Air fryer is an appliance that combines a number of functions into one, making cooking easier and faster. When you've mastered it, it opens up more doors for you as well as other opportunities. As soon as you have a firm grasp on the fundamentals and are comfortable using your Salter Air fryer, you are free to experiment with different techniques and make adjustments to the recipes as you see appropriate. The Salter Air fryer is capable of producing a wide variety of dishes, and you can even convert your go-to dish for the stovetop into one that works well in the air fryer by making some adjustments. It all comes down to the variety of choices available, isn't that, right?

It has never been simpler to cook meals that are both delicious and beneficial to one's health. It is quite clear that this collection of recipes substantiates its claims. Bon Appetite!

BREAKFAST RECIPES

Cheesy Baked Grits

PREP TIME: 10 MINUTES • COOKING TIME: 12 MINUTES • TOTAL COOKING TIME: 22 MINUTES • SERVES: 6

Ingredients

2 (1-ounce) packages instant grits (⅔ cup)
1 large egg, beaten
1 tablespoon butter, melted
2 cloves garlic, minced
½ to 1 teaspoon red pepper flakes
¾ cup hot water
1 cup shredded cheddar cheese or jalapeño Jack cheese

Direction

1 Combine the water, grits, egg, butter, garlic, and red pepper flakes in a heat-resistant 6-by-3-inch round pan. Stir until well combined. Stir in the cheese shreds.
2 Place the pan in the basket of the air fryer. Set the Salter air fryer to 400°F for 12 minutes, or until the grits have cooked through and a knife inserted near the center comes out clean.
3 Let stand for 5 minutes before serving.

Easy Mexican Shakshuka

PREP TIME: 5 MINUTES • COOKING TIME: 6 MINUTES • TOTAL COOKING TIME: 11 MINUTES • SERVES: 1

Ingredients

½ cup salsa
2 large eggs, room temperature
½ teaspoon fine sea salt
¼ teaspoon smoked paprika
⅛ teaspoon ground cumin
2 tablespoons cilantro leaves

Direction

1 Adjust the temperature of the Salter air fryer to 400 degrees Fahrenheit.
2 Place the salsa in an air fryer-compatible 6-inch pie plate or casserole dish. Cracked eggs are to be sprinkled with salt, paprika, and cumin after being added to salsa.

3 Place the pan in the air fryer and cook for 6 minutes, or until the egg whites are set and the yolks are cooked to your satisfaction. Remove from the air fryer and garnish with the cilantro before serving.

Air Fryer Hard-Boiled Eggs

PREP TIME: 1 MINUTE • COOKING TIME: 15 MINUTES • TOTAL COOKING TIME: 16 MINUTES• SERVES: 6

Ingredients

6 eggs

Direction

1 Place the eggs in the air fryer's basket. (You can place the eggs in an oven-safe bowl if you are anxious about them rolling around and breaking.)

2 Set the Salter AF's temperature to 250 degrees Fahrenheit. Prepare the oven and bake for 15 minutes with the timer set (if you prefer a soft-boiled egg, reduce the cook time to 10 minutes). Meanwhile, fill a medium mixing bowl half full of ice water. Use tongs to take the eggs from the air fryer basket, and transfer them to the ice water bath. Let the eggs sit for 5 minutes in the ice water.

3 Peel and consume immediately or refrigerate for up to one week.

Easy Air Fryer Baked Eggs with Cheese

PREP TIME: 2 MINUTES • COOKING TIME: 6 MINUTES • TOTAL COOKING TIME: 8 MINUTES •SERVES: 2

Ingredients

2 large eggs
2 tablespoons half-and-half, divided
2 teaspoons shredded Cheddar cheese, divided
Salt
Freshly ground black pepper

Direction

1 Lightly spray the insides of two (8-ounce) ramekins with cooking spray. Separate an egg per ramekin.

2 Each ramekin should contain 1 tablespoon of half-and-half and 1 teaspoon of cheese. Season with salt and pepper. Using a fork, stir the egg mixture. Set the ramekins in the air fryer basket.

3 Set the temperature of your Salter AF to 330°F. Set the timer for 6 minutes and bake.

4 Check to see if the eggs are cooked. If they are not done, heat for 1 minute more and check again.

Bacon-and-Eggs Avocado

PREP TIME: 5 MINUTES • COOKING TIME: 17 MINUTES

• TOTAL COOKING TIME: 22 MINUTES • SERVES: 1

Ingredients

1 avocado, halved, peeled, and pitted
2 slices bacon
Fresh parsley, for serving (optional)
1 large egg
Sea salt flakes, for garnish (optional)

Direction

1. Spray avocado oil on the Salter air fryer basket. Preheat the Salter air fryer to 320°F. Fill a small bowl with refreshing water.
2. Gently cook the egg: Place the egg in the air fryer basket. Cook for 6 minutes for a soft yolk or 7 minutes for a cooked yolk. Transfer the egg to the dish of cool water and let settle for 2 minutes. Peel and set aside. Use a spoon to carve out extra space in the center of the avocado halves until the cavities are big enough to fit the soft-boiled egg. Place the soft-boiled egg in the center of one avocado half and replace the other avocado half on top so that the avocado appears whole from the outside.
3. Starting at one end of the avocado, wrap the bacon around the avocado to thoroughly cover it. Utilize toothpicks to secure the bacon. Place the bacon-wrapped avocado in the Salter air fryer basket and cook for 5 minutes. Toast the avocado for an additional 5 minutes, or until the bacon is cooked to your liking. Serve on a bed of fresh parsley, if desired, and sprinkle with salt flakes, if desired.
4. Best served fresh. Refrigerate leftovers in an airtight container for up to four days. Reheat in a preheated air fryer at 320°F for four minutes, or until thoroughly heated.

Double-Dipped Mini Cinnamon Biscuits

PREP TIME: 15 MINUTES • COOKING TIME: 13 MINUTES
• TOTAL COOKING TIME: 28 MINUTES • SERVES: 8 BISCUITS

Ingredients

½ teaspoon fine sea salt
¼ cup unsweetened, unflavored almond milk
1 large egg
1 teaspoon vanilla extract
3 teaspoons ground cinnamon
½ cup Swerve confectioners'-style sweetener or equivalent amount of powdered sweetener
¼ cup heavy cream or unsweetened, unflavored almond milk
2 cups blanched almond flour
½ cup Swerve confectioners'-style sweetener or equivalent amount of liquid or powdered sweetener
1 teaspoon baking powder

¼ cup plus 2 tablespoons (¾ stick) very cold unsalted butter

Direction

1. Adjust the temperature of the Salter air fryer to 350 degrees Fahrenheit. Line an air fryer-compatible pie dish with parchment paper.
2. In a medium-sized bowl, mix together the almond flour, sweetener (if powdered; do not add liquid sweetener), baking powder, and salt. Cut the butter into ½-inch squares, then use a hand mixer to work the butter into the dry ingredients. When you are done, the mixture should still have chunks of butter.
3. In a small dish, mix together the almond milk, egg, and vanilla extract (if using liquid sweetener, add it as well) until incorporated. Mix the wet ingredients into the dry ingredients using a fork until large clumps form. Incorporate the cinnamon into the dough using your hands. Form the dough into sixteen 1-inch balls and place them on the prepared pan, spacing them about ½ inch apart. (If you're using a smaller air fryer, work in batches if necessary.)
4. Bake in the air fryer until golden, 10 to 13 minutes. Remove from the air fryer and let cool on the pan for at least 5 minutes.
5. While the biscuits bake, make the glaze: In a small bowl, combine the powdered sweetener and heavy cream while stirring with a fork. When the biscuits have partly cooled, dip the tops into the glaze, let it dry little, and then dip again to form a thick glaze. Serve at room temperature or warm. Refrigerate unglazed biscuits in an airtight container for up to three days or freeze them for up to one month. Reheat in a preheated air fryer at 350 degrees Fahrenheit for five minutes, or until thoroughly heated, and dip in the glaze as instructed above.

Foolproof Air Fryer Bacon

PREP TIME: 5 MINUTES • COOKING TIME: 10 MINUTES • TOTAL COOKING TIME: 15 MINUTES •SERVES: 5

Ingredients

10 slices bacon

Direction

1. For the bacon slices to fit in the air fryer, they must be cut in half.
2. Place the half-slices in a single layer in the fryer basket. (You may need to fry the bacon in more than one batch.)
3. Set the Salter AF's temperature to 400 degrees Fahrenheit. Set the timer and fry for 5 minutes. Open the drawer and check the bacon. (The power of the fan may have caused the bacon to fly around during the cooking process. Use a fork or tongs to adjust the slices if necessary.)
4. Reset the timer and fry for 5 minutes more. After the time has passed, recheck the bacon. If you like your bacon crispier, cook it for another 1 to 2 minutes.

Meritage Eggs

PREP TIME: 5 MINUTES • COOKING TIME: 8 MINUTES • TOTAL COOKING TIME: 13 MINUTES • SERVES: 2

Ingredients

2 teaspoons unsalted butter (or coconut oil for dairy-free), for greasing the ramekins
4 large eggs
2 teaspoons chopped fresh thyme
½ teaspoon fine sea salt
¼ teaspoon ground black pepper
2 tablespoons heavy cream (or unsweetened, unflavored almond milk for dairy-free)
3 tablespoons finely grated Parmesan
Fresh thyme leaves, for garnish (optional)

Direction

1. Adjust the temperature of the Salter air fryer to 400 degrees Fahrenheit. Prepare two 4-ounce ramekins with butter; set aside. Crack 2 eggs into each ramekin and divide the thyme, salt, and pepper between the ramekins. Pour 1 tablespoon of heavy cream into the bottom of each ramekin. Sprinkle each ramekin with 1½ tablespoons of the Parmesan cheese.
2. Place the ramekins in the air fryer and cook for 8 minutes for soft-cooked yolks (longer if you desire a harder yolk). Garnish with a sprinkle of ground black pepper and thyme leaves, if desired. Freshest served.

Easy Air Fryer Buttermilk Biscuits

PREP TIME: 5 MINUTES • COOKING TIME: 5 MINUTES • TOTAL COOKING TIME: 10 MINUTES • SERVES: 12

Ingredients

2 cups all-purpose flour
1 tablespoon baking powder
¼ teaspoon baking soda
2 teaspoons sugar
1 teaspoon salt
6 tablespoons (¾ stick) cold unsalted butter, cut into 1-tablespoon slices
¾ cup buttermilk
4 tablespoons (½ stick) unsalted butter, melted (optional)

Direction

1. Spray the basket of the Salter air fryer with olive oil.
2. Mix together the flour, baking powder, baking soda, sugar, and salt in a large mixing bowl.
3. Cut the butter into the flour with a fork until the mixture resembles coarse meal.
4. Add the buttermilk and mix until smooth. Sprinkle flour on a clean work surface. Turn the dough out onto the work surface and roll it out until it is about ½ inch thick.
5. Using a 2-inch biscuit cutter, cut the biscuits into individual shapes. Place the uncooked biscuits in the oiled Salter air fryer basket in a single layer.

6 Set the Salter AF's temperature to 360 degrees Fahrenheit. Set the timer for 5 minutes and bake.
7 Place the cooked biscuits on a platter from the air fryer. Brush the tops with melted butter, if desired. Cut the remaining biscuits (you may have to gather up the scraps of dough and reroll the dough for the last couple of biscuits). Bake the remaining biscuits.
8 Plating, serving, and enjoying!

Breakfast Pizza

PREP TIME: 5 MINUTES • COOKING TIME: 8 MINUTES • TOTAL COOKING TIME: 13 MINUTES • SERVES: 1

Ingredients

¼ cup unsweetened, unflavored almond milk
¼ teaspoon fine sea salt
⅛ teaspoon ground black pepper
¼ cup diced onions
¼ cup shredded Parmesan cheese
6 pepperoni slices
¼ teaspoon dried oregano leaves
2 large eggs
¼ cup pizza sauce, warmed, for serving

Direction

1 Heat the Salter air fryer to 350 degrees Fahrenheit before use. Grease a three by six-inch cake pan.
2 In a small bowl, use a fork to mix together the eggs, almond milk, salt, and pepper. Stir the onions into the mixture. Pour the mixture into the buttered pan. Top with the cheese (if using), pepperoni slices (if using), and oregano.
3 Place the pan in the air fryer and cook for 8 minutes, or until the eggs are cooked to your liking.
4 With a spatula, loosen the eggs from the pan's sides and place them on a serving plate. Drizzle the pizza sauce on top. Freshest served.

Easy Bacon

PREP TIME: 2 MINUTES • COOKING TIME: 6 MINUTES • TOTAL COOKING TIME: 8 MINUTES • SERVES: 2

Ingredients

4 slices thin-cut bacon or beef bacon

Direction

1 Spray some avocado oil onto the basket of the Salter air fryer. Put the Salter air fryer into the "360 degrees Fahrenheit" setting on the temperature dial.
2 Place the bacon in the basket of the Salter air fryer in a single layer, leaving approximately 14 inch of space between each piece, and set the timer for 4 to 6 minutes (thicker bacon will take longer). After four minutes, check to see if the bacon is being overcooked by removing it from

the oven.

3 The most recent ingredients available. The leftovers can be stored in the refrigerator for up to four days in an airtight container. Reheat in an air fryer that has been preheated to 360 degrees Fahrenheit for two minutes, or until the food is hot throughout.

Blueberry Pancake Poppers

PREP TIME: 5 MINUTES • COOKING TIME: 8 MINUTES • TOTAL COOKING TIME: 13 MINUTES • SERVES: 8

Ingredients

1 tablespoon sugar
1 teaspoon baking soda
½ teaspoon baking powder
1 cup milk
1 large egg
1 teaspoon vanilla extract
1 teaspoon olive oil
1 cup all-purpose flour
½ cup fresh blueberries

Direction

1 Flour, sugar, baking soda, and baking powder should all be mixed together in a medium-sized mixing dish. Combine the milk, egg, vanilla, and vegetable oil. Spray some cooking spray on the inside of a muffin tin that will be used in an air fryer. Put two-thirds of the batter into each muffin cup. (It is possible that you will require baking the poppers in more than one batch.) Place a handful of blueberries in each of the muffin cups.

2 Put the muffin tin inside of the basket of the air fryer.

3 Adjust the temperature on the Salter AF so that it reads 320 degrees Fahrenheit. Bake the dish after setting the timer for eight minutes. Put a toothpick through the middle of a pancake popper, and if it comes out clean, the pancake poppers are ready to be eaten. If the batter sticks to the toothpick, give the poppers an additional two minutes of cooking time and then check them again. After the poppers have finished cooking, remove the muffin tin from the air fryer basket using silicone oven mitts in order to avoid burning your hands. Remove the poppers from the pan and place them on a wire rack to cool.

Air Fryer Cinnamon Rolls

PREP TIME: 5 MINUTES • COOKING TIME: 12 MINUTES • TOTAL COOKING TIME: 17 MINUTES • SERVES: 1

Ingredients

1 can of cinnamon rolls

Direction

1 Spray the basket of the Salter air fryer with olive oil.

2 Separate the cinnamon rolls from their packaging and place them in the air fryer basket.

3 2
4 Set the temperature of your Salter AF to 340°F. Set the timer for 6 minutes and bake.
5 Use tongs to turn the cinnamon rolls. Reset the timer and bake for another 6 minutes.
6 When the rolls are done cooking, use tongs to remove them from the air fryer. Transfer the cookies to a tray and frost them with the frosting included in the container.

Denver Omelet

PREP TIME: 5 MINUTES • COOKING TIME: 8 MINUTES • TOTAL COOKING TIME: 13 MINUTES • SERVES: 1

Ingredients

¼ cup unsweetened, unflavored almond milk
¼ teaspoon fine sea salt
⅛ teaspoon ground black pepper
¼ cup diced ham (omit for vegetarian)
¼ cup diced green and red bell peppers
2 tablespoons diced green onions, plus more for garnish
¼ cup shredded cheddar cheese
2 large eggs
Quartered cherry tomatoes, for serving

Direction

1 Heat the Salter air fryer to 350 degrees Fahrenheit before use. Coat a six-by-three-inch cake pan with cooking spray. In a small bowl, use a fork to whisk together the eggs, almond milk, salt, and pepper. Add the ham, bell peppers, and green onions. Pour the mixture into the buttered pan. Add the cheese on top (if using).
2 Place the pan in the basket of the air fryer. Cook for eight minutes, or until the eggs have reached the desired doneness. With a spatula, take the omelet from the pan and arrange it on a serving platter. Garnish with green onions and serve with cherry tomatoes, if desired. Freshest served.

Homemade Air Fried Banana Bread

PREP TIME: 5 MINUTES • COOKING TIME: 22 MINUTES • TOTAL COOKING TIME: 13 MINUTES • SERVES: 3

Ingredients

1 teaspoon baking soda
3 ripe bananas, mashed
1 cup sugar
4 tablespoons (½ stick) unsalted butter, melted
1½ cups all-purpose flour
1 large egg
1 teaspoon salt

Direction

1. Cooking spray should be applied to three miniature loaf pans. Combine the sugar and bananas in a large mixing bowl. In a separate large mixing bowl, combine the egg, butter, flour, baking soda, and salt and mix well. Add the banana mixture to the egg and flour mixture. Mix well. Divide the batter evenly among the prepared pans.
2. Set the tiny loaf pans into the air fryer basket.
3. Adjust the temperature of the Salter AF to 310 degrees Fahrenheit. Set the timer and bake for 22 minutes. If a toothpick inserted into the center of each loaf comes out clean, the loaves are done. If the batter clings to the toothpick, cook the loaves for 2 minutes more and check again. When the loaves are cooked through, use silicone oven mitts to remove the pans from the air fryer basket. Turn out the loaves onto a wire rack to cool.

Air Fryer Homemade Blueberry Muffins

PREP TIME: 5 MINUTES • COOKING TIME: 14 MINUTES • TOTAL COOKING TIME: 19 MINUTES • SERVES: 10

Ingredients

2/3 cup all-purpose flour
1 teaspoon baking powder
2 tablespoons sugar
1 egg
2 teaspoons vanilla extract
1/3 cup low-fat milk
3 tablespoons unsalted butter, melted
3/4 cup fresh blueberries

Direction

1. In a medium mixing bowl, combine the flour, baking powder, sugar, egg, vanilla, milk, and melted butter. Incorporate the blueberries. Coat the interior of a muffin tin for an air fryer with cooking spray. Fill each muffin cup to roughly two-thirds capacity. Insert the muffin tin into the basket of the air fryer.
2. Set the Salter AF's temperature to 320 degrees Fahrenheit. Set the timer and bake for 14 minutes.
3. If a toothpick inserted into the center of a muffin comes out clean, the muffins are done. If batter adheres to the toothpick, bake the muffins for two additional minutes and recheck. When the muffins are thoroughly cooked, remove the muffin pan from the air fryer basket using silicone oven mitts. Before serving, place the muffins on a wire rack to cool slightly.

VEGAN RECIPES

Air Fryer Asparagus

PREP TIME: 5 MINUTES • COOKING TIME: 8 MINUTES • TOTAL COOKING TIME: 13 MINUTES • SERVES: 2

Ingredients

Olive oil non-stick spray
Nutritional yeast
One bunch of asparagus

Direction

1. After washing asparagus, its woody ends should be clipped. Spray asparagus with olive oil and sprinkle with yeast.
2. Arrange asparagus in a single layer in your Air fryer. Set the temperature and time to 360°F and 8 minutes, respectively, on your Salter AF.

Simple Roasted Garlic Asparagus

PREP TIME: 5 MINUTES • COOKING TIME: 10 MINUTES • TOTAL COOKING TIME: 15 MINUTES • SERVES: 4

Ingredients

1 pound asparagus
2 tablespoons olive oil
1 tablespoon balsamic vinegar
2 teaspoons minced garlic
Salt
Freshly ground black pepper

Direction

1. Remove the tips of the asparagus spears that are white in color.
2. In a large bowl, combine the asparagus, olive oil, vinegar, garlic, salt, and pepper.
3. Using your hands, gently incorporate all of the ingredients, coating the asparagus thoroughly. Place the asparagus in the Salter air fryer's basket or on an air fryer-sized baking sheet placed in the basket.
4. Set the temperature of the Salter AF to 400 degrees Fahrenheit. Set a timer for five minutes, then roast the meat.
5. Utilize tongs to rotate the asparagus. Reset the timer and cook for an additional five minutes.

Ranch Kale Chips

PREP TIME: 5 MINUTES • COOKING TIME: 10 MINUTES • TOTAL COOKING TIME: 15 MINUTES • SERVES: 8 CUPS

Ingredients

½ teaspoon dried chives
½ teaspoon dried dill weed
½ teaspoon dried parsley
¼ teaspoon garlic powder
¼ teaspoon onion powder
⅛ teaspoon fine sea salt
⅛ teaspoon ground black pepper
2 large bunches kale

Direction

1. Spray avocado oil on the Salter air fryer basket. Preheat the Salter air fryer at 360 degrees Fahrenheit.
2. In a small bowl, mix together the spices, salt, and pepper. Thoroughly wash and pat dry the kale. Using a sharp knife, remove the thick inner stems, then spray the leaves with avocado oil and sprinkle them with the spice blend.
3. Place the kale leaves in the air fryer in a single layer and cook for ten minutes, tossing and turning the chips halfway through cooking. Put the chips on a baking sheet to cool and get crisp. Proceed with the remaining kale. If desired, sprinkle salt over the chips before serving.
4. If stored at room temperature for up to one week in an airtight container, kale chips should be consumed within three days.

Almond Flour Battered And Crisped Onion Rings

PREP TIME: 5 MINUTES • COOKING TIME: 15 MINUTES • TOTAL COOKING TIME: 20 MINUTES • SERVES: 3

Ingredients

½ cup almond flour
¾ cup coconut milk
1 big white onion, sliced into rings
1 egg, beaten
1 tablespoon baking powder
1 tablespoon smoked paprika
Salt and pepper to taste

Direction

1. The Salter air fryer should be preheated for five minutes. In a mixing bowl, combine the almond flour, baking powder, smoked paprika, salt, and pepper. Separately, whisk together the eggs and coconut milk in a separate bowl. Soak the onion pieces in the egg mixture.
2. Coat the sliced onion with the flour mixture.

3 Place in the air fryer's basket. Close the oven and cook for 15 minutes at 325 degrees.
4 Shake the fryer basket midway during the cooking time to ensure that the food is evenly fried.

Crispy Nacho Avocado Fries

PREP TIME: 10 MINUTES • COOKING TIME: 15 MINUTES • TOTAL COOKING TIME: 25 MINUTES • SERVES: 6

Ingredients

3 firm, barely ripe avocados, halved, peeled, and pitted
2 cups pork dust
2 teaspoons fine sea salt
2 teaspoons ground black pepper
2 teaspoons ground cumin
1 teaspoon chili powder
1 teaspoon paprika
½ teaspoon garlic powder
½ teaspoon onion powder
2 large eggs
Salsa, for serving (optional)
Fresh chopped cilantro leaves, for garnish (optional)

Direction

1 Spray avocado oil on the Salter air fryer basket. Adjust the temperature of the Salter air fryer to 400 degrees Fahrenheit.
2 The avocados are sliced in the shape of french fries. In a bowl, combine the pork dust, salt, pepper, and spices. In a small bowl, beat the eggs individually.
3 The avocado fries are coated in beaten eggs, swirled to remove excess, and then dipped in a mixture of pork dust and seasoning. Apply the breading with your hands to each fry.
4 Spray the fries with avocado oil and arrange them in a single layer in the basket of the Salter air fryer, leaving room in between. If there are too many fries for a single layer, work in batches.
5 13 to 15 minutes in the air fryer, turning after 5 minutes, until golden brown.
6 If desired, serve with salsa and garnish with chopped fresh cilantro. Freshest ingredients served. Refrigerate leftovers for up to five days in an airtight container. Reheat at 400 degrees Fahrenheit for three minutes in an air fryer that has been warmed.

Chermoula-Roasted Beets

PREP TIME: 15 MINUTES • COOKING TIME: 25 MINUTES • TOTAL COOKING TIME: 40 MINUTES • SERVES: 4

Ingredients

1 cup packed fresh cilantro leaves
½ cup packed fresh parsley leaves
6 cloves garlic, peeled

2 teaspoons smoked paprika
2 teaspoons ground cumin
1 teaspoon ground coriander
½ to 1 teaspoon cayenne pepper
Pinch crushed saffron (optional)
½ cup extra-virgin olive oil
Kosher salt
For the Beets
3 medium beets, trimmed, peeled, and cut into 1-inch chunks
2 tablespoons chopped fresh cilantro
2 tablespoons chopped fresh parsley

Direction

1. In a food processor, combine the cilantro, parsley, garlic, paprika, cumin, coriander, and cayenne for the chermoula. Crush until coarsely chopped. If using, add the saffron and mix until well incorporated. While the food processor is running, add the olive oil in a slow, steady stream; process until the sauce is homogenous. season to taste with salt.
2. In a large bowl, drizzle enough chermoula to coat the beets with 12 cups.
3. Place the beets in the air fryer's basket. Adjust the temperature of the Salter air fryer to 375 degrees Fahrenheit for 25 minutes, or until the beets are tender. Transfer the beets to a serving dish. Serve with chopped cilantro and parsley as garnishes.

Jalapeño Poppers

PREP TIME: 10 MINUTES • COOKING TIME: 10 MINUTES • TOTAL COOKING TIME: 20 MINUTES • SERVES: 4

Ingredients

1/2 cup fine cornmeal
12-18 whole fresh jalapeño
1 cup nonfat refried beans
1 cup shredded Monterey Jack or extra-sharp cheddar cheese
1 scallion, sliced
1 teaspoon salt, divided
1/4 cup all-purpose flour
2 large eggs
Olive oil or canola oil cooking spray

Direction

1. Start by slicing each jalapeo lengthwise on one side. Place the jalapeos side-by-side in a microwave-safe bowl and microwave them for about 5 minutes, or until they are considerably softened. While the jalapeos cook, combine refried beans, scallions, 1/2 teaspoon of salt, and cheese in a bowl. Once the jalapeo peppers have softened, remove the seeds and add one spoonful of the bean mixture. Apply pressure on the jalapeo to seal

the filling within. In a small bowl, the eggs should be beaten, and in a second basin, the flour should be placed. In a different bowl, combine the remaining salt with the remaining cornmeal. Carefully dip each pepper with flour, then egg, and then cornmeal, ensuring that each pepper is completely covered. Place the peppers on a flat surface and coat them with an olive oil-based cooking spray.

2 Cook peppers at 400 degrees Fahrenheit for 5 minutes, then flip and cook for an additional 5 minutes; serve hot.

Fried Plantains

PREP TIME: 10 MINUTES • COOKING TIME: 8 MINUTES • TOTAL COOKING TIME: 18 MINUTES • SERVES: 2

Ingredients

2 ripe plantains, peeled and cut at a diagonal into ½-inch-thick pieces
3 tablespoons ghee, melted
¼ teaspoon kosher salt

Direction

1 In a medium bowl, toss the plantains with the ghee and salt.

2 Place the plantain pieces in the air fryer's basket. Set the air fryer to 400 degrees Fahrenheit for 8 minutes. The plantains are done when the interior is soft and tender and the exterior is crisp, sweet, and brown.

Bacon-Wrapped Asparagus

PREP TIME: 5 MINUTES • COOKING TIME: 10 MINUTES • TOTAL COOKING TIME: 15 MINUTES • SERVES: 4

Ingredients

4 slices bacon or beef bacon
½ cup Ranch Dressin for serving
1 pound asparagus, trimmed (about 24 spears)
3 tablespoons chopped fresh chives, for garnish

Direction

1 Spray avocado oil on the Salter air fryer basket. Adjust the temperature of the Salter air fryer to 400 degrees Fahrenheit.

2 Create long, thin bacon strips by slicing the bacon down the middle. Wrap one slice of bacon around three asparagus spears and secure with toothpicks. Continue with the remainder of the asparagus and bacon.

3 Place the asparagus bundles in the air fryer in a single layer. Using a more compact air fryer may need cooking in batches. Cook until the asparagus ends are gently browned and the bacon is crisp, approximately 8 minutes for thin stalks and 10 minutes for medium to thick stalks.

4 Garnish with ranch dressing and chopped chives. Freshest ingredients served.

Air Fried Roasted Corn on The Cob

PREP TIME: 5 MINUTES • COOKING TIME: 10 MINUTES • TOTAL COOKING TIME: 15 MINUTES • SERVES: 4

Ingredients

4 ears of corn, husks and silk removed
Unsalted butter, for topping
Salt, for topping
1 tablespoon vegetable oil
Freshly ground black pepper, for topping

Direction

1. Rub the vegetable oil into the corn kernels to completely coat them.
2. Set the temperature of the Salter AF to 400 degrees Fahrenheit. Set the timer for 5 minutes on the grill.
3. Using tongs, flip or rotate the corn.
4. Reset the timer and continue grilling for another 5 minutes.
5. The dish should be accompanied by a pat of butter and a generous amount of salt and pepper.

Parmesan Breaded Zucchini Chips

PREP TIME: 15 MINUTES • COOKING TIME: 20 MINUTES • TOTAL COOKING TIME: 35 MINUTES • SERVES: 5

Ingredients

Salt
Pepper
2 medium zucchini
2 eggs
⅓ cup bread crumbs
⅓ cup grated Parmesan cheese
Salt
Pepper
½ cup mayonnaise
½ tablespoon olive oil
Juice of ½ lemon
1 teaspoon minced garlic
Cooking oil

Direction

1. Using a knife or mandoline, slice the zucchini into thin chips (about 1/8 inch thick). In a

small bowl, beat the eggs. In a separate small bowl, combine the bread crumbs, Parmesan cheese, and salt and pepper to taste. Spray cooking oil onto the basket of the Salter air fryer. Individually dipping the zucchini pieces in the egg mixture and then the bread crumb mixture. You may alternatively sprinkle the bread crumbs on the zucchini slices with a spoon. Do not stack the zucchini chips within the Air fryer's basket.

2 Cook in increments. Cooking oil is sprayed from a distance on the chips (otherwise, the breading may fly off). Prepare yourself for ten minutes. Repeat step 5 with the remaining zucchini chips.

In a separate bowl, combine the mayonnaise, olive oil, lemon juice, and garlic while the zucchini is cooking. Season with salt and pepper to taste. All ingredients must be well combined. Serve cooled zucchini with the aioli.

Green Beans & Bacon

PREP TIME: 10 MINUTES • COOKING TIME: 20 MINUTES • TOTAL COOKING TIME: 35 MINUTES • SERVES: 4

Ingredients

3 cups frozen cut green beans
¼ cup water
1 medium onion, chopped
3 slices bacon, chopped
Kosher salt and black pepper

Direction

1 In a circular 6-by-3-inch heat-resistant pan, combine the frozen green beans, onion, bacon, and water. Toss to combine. Place the pan in the air fryer's basket.
2 15 minutes at 375 degrees Fahrenheit and 375 degrees Fahrenheit.
3 Increase the air fryer's temperature to 400 degrees Fahrenheit for 5 minutes. Salt and pepper the beans to taste, then combine thoroughly.
4 Remove the pan from the basket of the Salter air fryer and cover with aluminum foil. Before serving, allow the beans to settle for five minutes.

Bell Pepper-Corn Wrapped in Tortilla

PREP TIME: 5 MINUTES • COOKING TIME: 15 MINUTES • TOTAL COOKING TIME: 20 MINUTES • SERVES: 4

Ingredients

1 small red bell pepper, chopped
1 small yellow onion, diced
1 tablespoon water
2 cobs grilled corn kernels
4 large tortillas

4 pieces commercial vegan nuggets, chopped
mixed greens for garnish

Direction

1. Adjust the temperature of the Salter air fryer to 400 degrees Fahrenheit. In a pan over medium heat, sauté the vegan nuggets with the onions, bell peppers, and corn kernels in water. Set aside.
2. Fill corn tortillas with filling.
3. Cook the tortillas in an air fryer for 15 minutes, or until they are crisp. Serve atop a bed of greens.

Bloomin' Onion

PREP TIME: 10 MINUTES • COOKING TIME: 35 MINUTES • TOTAL COOKING TIME: 45 MINUTES • SERVES: 8

Ingredients

1 extra-large onion
2 large eggs
1 tablespoon water
½ cup powdered Parmesan cheese
2 teaspoons paprika
1 teaspoon garlic powder
¼ teaspoon cayenne pepper
¼ teaspoon ground black pepper
FOR GARNISH (OPTIONAL):
Fresh parsley leaves
Powdered Parmesan cheese
FOR SERVING (OPTIONAL):
Prepared yellow mustard
Ranch Dressing
¼ teaspoon fine sea salt
Reduced-sugar or sugar-free ketchup

Direction

1. Spray avocado oil on the Salter air fryer basket. Preheat the Salter air fryer at 350 degrees Fahrenheit.
2. Using a sharp knife, remove the onion's outer covering and the top half-inch. Cut the onion into eight equal pieces, stopping 1 inch from the base to preserve the onion's integrity. Spread the pieces, or "petals," carefully apart.
3. In a large bowl, crack the eggs and whisk in the water. In a dish, place the onion and thoroughly coat it with egg. Coat the center and all petals of the onion with a spoon.
4. In a small bowl, combine the Parmesan, spices, salt, and pepper.
5. Place the onion in a 6-inch pie pan or casserole dish. Sprinkle the seasoning mixture over the onion and work it into the petals using your fingertips. Avocado oil is drizzled on the onion.

6 Cover the onion with parchment paper and then aluminum foil in a loose fashion.
7 Place the dish within an air fryer. Remove the food from the air fryer after 30 minutes and increase the temperature to 400 degrees Fahrenheit.
8 Remove the aluminum foil and parchment paper, and spray the onion once more with avocado oil. Transfer the onion to the air fryer basket, using oven-safe gloves or a tea towel to protect your hands. Cook for a further 3 to 5 minutes, or until golden and crisp.
9 Garnish, if desired, with fresh parsley and Parmesan powder. Served with mustard, ranch dressing, and ketchup, if desired.
10 Keep leftovers in an airtight jar in the refrigerator for up to four days. Warm and crisp in an air fryer heated to 400 degrees Fahrenheit for three to five minutes.

Mexican Corn In A Cup

PREP TIME: 5 MINUTES • COOKING TIME: 10 MINUTES • TOTAL COOKING TIME: 15 MINUTES • SERVES: 4

Ingredients

4 cups (32-ounce bag) frozen corn kernels (do not thaw)
Vegetable oil spray
2 tablespoons butter
¼ cup sour cream
¼ cup mayonnaise
¼ cup grated Parmesan cheese (or feta, cotija, or queso fresco)
2 tablespoons fresh lemon or lime juice
1 teaspoon chili powder
Chopped fresh green onion (optional)
Chopped fresh cilantro (optional)

Direction

1 Before adding the corn, coat the bottom of the Salter air fryer basket with vegetable oil spray.
2 Ten minutes at 350 degrees Fahrenheit and 350 degrees Fahrenheit.
3 Transfer the corn to a serving basin. Stir butter in until melted. Mix the sour cream, mayonnaise, cheese, lemon juice, and chili powder thoroughly. Serve immediately with green onion and cilantro (if using).

Air Fried Honey Roasted Carrots

PREP TIME: 5 MINUTES • COOKING TIME: 12 MINUTES • TOTAL COOKING TIME: 17 MINUTES • SERVES: 4

Ingredients

3 cups baby carrots
1 tablespoon extra-virgin olive oil
1 tablespoon honey
Salt

Freshly ground black pepper
Fresh dill (optional)

Direction

1. In a large bowl, combine the carrots, olive oil, honey, salt, and pepper. Make sure the carrots are well coated with oil. Place the carrots in the air fryer's basket.
2. Adjust the temperature of the Salter AF to 390 degrees Fahrenheit. Prepare the veggies for 12 minutes, or until they are fork-tender.
3. Remove the air fryer drawer to release the air fryer basket. If preferred, pour the carrots into a bowl, sprinkle with dill, and serve.

Crispy Sesame-Ginger Broccoli

PREP TIME: 10 MINUTES • COOKING TIME: 15 MINUTES • TOTAL COOKING TIME: 25 MINUTES • SERVES: 4

Ingredients

3 tablespoons toasted sesame oil
2 teaspoons sesame seeds
1 tablespoon chili-garlic sauce
2 teaspoons minced fresh ginger
½ teaspoon kosher salt
½ teaspoon black pepper
1 (16-ounce) package frozen broccoli florets (do not thaw)

Direction

1. In a large bowl, combine the sesame oil, sesame seeds, chili-garlic sauce, ginger, salt, and pepper. Stir until completely combined. Add the broccoli and toss to evenly coat.
2. Arrange the broccoli in the air fryer's basket. Set the Salter air fryer to 325 degrees Fahrenheit for 15 minutes, or until the broccoli is crisp, tender, and the edges are lightly toasted, carefully rotating the broccoli halfway through cooking.

POULTRY RECIPES

Korean Chicken Wings

PREP TIME: 5 MINUTES • COOKING TIME: 10 MINUTES • TOTAL COOKING TIME: 15 MINUTES • SERVES: 8

Ingredients

1 tsp. pepper
1 tsp. salt
2 pounds chicken wings
2 packets Splenda
1 tbsp. minced garlic
1 tbsp. minced ginger
1 tbsp. sesame oil
1 tsp. agave nectar
1 tbsp. mayo
2 tbsp. gochujang
¼ C. chopped green onions
2 tsp. sesame seeds

Direction:

1 Ensure the air fryer has reached a temperature of 400 degrees Fahrenheit.
2 Place a rack on a small pan lined with aluminum foil, and then place the pan and the rack in an air fryer.
3 Pepper and salt the wings, then set them on the rack.
4 Set the temperature to 160 degrees Fahrenheit and the timer to 20 minutes. Air fry for 20 minutes, flipping after 10 minutes. As chicken is air-fried, combine the sauce ingredients.
5 When the internal temperature of the chicken reaches 160 degrees, remove the wings and set them in a bowl. Pour half of the sauce mixture over the chicken wings and toss to evenly coat. Return covered wings to the air fryer for five minutes, or until the temperature reaches 165 degrees Fahrenheit. Remove and garnish with scallions and sesame seeds. Dip into more sauce.

Buffalo Chicken Wings

PREP TIME: 10 MINUTES • COOKING TIME: 24 MINUTES • TOTAL COOKING TIME: 34 MINUTES • SERVES: 4

Ingredients

8 tablespoons (1 stick) unsalted butter, melted
½ cup hot sauce

2 tablespoons white vinegar
2 teaspoons Worcestershire sauce
1 teaspoon garlic powder
½ cup all-purpose flour
16 frozen chicken wings

Direction:

1 The air fryer should be preheated to 370 degrees Fahrenheit.
2 Over low heat, combine the butter, spicy sauce, vinegar, Worcestershire sauce, and garlic in a small saucepan. Stir well, then bring to a simmer.
3 Pour the flour into a mixing basin of medium size. Flour the chicken wings thoroughly.
4 Place the flour-coated wings in the basket of an air fryer.
5 Set the timer for 12 minutes and fry the food. The wings are turned with tongs.
6 Reset the timer and cook for a further 12 minutes.
7 Remove the basket from the drawer of the Salter air fryer. Place the chicken wings in a large mixing bowl and pour the sauce on top.
8 Serve with pleasure.

Almond Flour Coco-Milk Battered Chicken

PREP TIME: 5 MINUTES • COOKING TIME: 30 MINUTES • TOTAL COOKING TIME: 35 MINUTES • SERVES: 4

Ingredients

½ cup almond flour
1 ½ tablespoons old bay Cajun seasoning
1 egg, beaten
4 small chicken thighs
¼ cup coconut milk
Salt and pepper to taste

Direction:

1 The Salter air fryer should be preheated for five minutes. Combine the egg and coconut milk in a bowl.
2 Soak the chicken thighs in the egg mixture that's been beaten. Combine almond flour, Cajun spice, salt, and pepper in a mixing bowl. The chicken thighs are dredged in the almond flour mixture. Place in the basket of an air fryer.
3 Cook for 30 minutes at 350 degrees Fahrenheit.

Harissa-Rubbed Cornish Game Hens

PREP TIME: 10 MINUTES • COOKING TIME: 20 MINUTES • TOTAL COOKING TIME: 60 MINUTES • SERVES: 4

Ingredients

For the Harissa
½ cup olive oil
6 cloves garlic, minced
2 tablespoons smoked paprika
1 tablespoon ground coriander
1 tablespoon ground cumin
1 teaspoon ground caraway
1 teaspoon kosher salt
½ to 1 teaspoon cayenne pepper
For the Hens
½ cup yogurt
Cornish game hens, any giblets removed, split in half lengthwise

Direction:

1 In a medium microwave-safe bowl, combine the oil, garlic, paprika, coriander, cumin, caraway, salt, and cayenne pepper for the harissa. Microwave for one minute at high power while stirring halfway through. (This can also be heated on the burner until the oil is boiling and hot. Or, if you must use your air fryer for everything, cook the paste at 350°F for 5 to 6 minutes, or until it is thoroughly heated.)

2 For the poultry: Combine 1 to 2 tablespoons harissa and yogurt in a small bowl. Whisk until thoroughly mixed. Pour the marinade over the chicken halves within a resealable plastic bag. Seal the bag and massage the contents until every piece is evenly coated. Marinate for 30 minutes at room temperature or up to 24 hours in the refrigerator.

3 2 Place the chicken halves in the air fryer basket in a single layer. (If your air fryer is smaller, you may need to cook the food in two batches.) 20 minutes at 400 degrees Fahrenheit at 400 degrees Fahrenheit. Make sure the game hens have reached the desired internal temperature by using a meat thermometer.

Parmesan Chicken Tenders

PREP TIME: 5 MINUTES • COOKING TIME: 8 MINUTES • TOTAL COOKING TIME: 13 MINUTES • SERVES: 4

Ingredients

1 pound chicken tenderloins
3 large egg whites
½ cup Italian-style bread crumbs
¼ cup grated Parmesan cheese

Direction:

1. Spray the basket of the Salter air fryer with olive oil. Remove any visible white fat from the chicken tenders. Whisk the egg whites in a small bowl until they become

frothy. Separately, combine the bread crumbs and Parmesan cheese in a small mixing dish. Blend well. The chicken tenders should be dipped in the egg mixture, followed by the Parmesan and bread crumbs. Remove any excess breadcrumbs. Place the chicken tenders in a single layer in the oiled basket of the Salter air fryer. Spray the chicken with olive oil liberally to prevent a dusty, undercooked coating.

2. Adjust the temperature of the Salter AF to 370 degrees Fahrenheit. Set the timer for 4 minutes and bake. Flip the chicken tenders with tongs and bake for a further 4 minutes. Verify that the chicken's interior temperature has reached 165 degrees Fahrenheit. Add cooking time as necessary. When the chicken is thoroughly done, plate it, serve it, and savor it.

Air Fryer Grilled Chicken Fajitas

PREP TIME: 10 MINUTES • COOKING TIME: 14 MINUTES • TOTAL COOKING TIME: 24 MINUTES • SERVES: 4

Ingredients

1 pound chicken tenders
1 onion, sliced
1 yellow bell pepper, diced
1 red bell pepper, diced
1 orange bell pepper, diced
2 tablespoons olive oil
1 tablespoon fajita seasoning mix

Direction:

1 Cut the chicken into thin pieces. In a large bowl, mix together the chicken, onion, and peppers. The chicken and vegetables should be evenly covered with olive oil and fajita seasoning. Place the chicken and vegetable mixture in a single layer in the basket of the Salter air fryer.
2 Set the Salter AF's temperature to 350 degrees Fahrenheit. Set the grill timer for 7 minutes.
3 Shake the basket and flip the chicken with tongs. Reset the timer and broil the chicken for an additional 7 minutes, or until the juices flow clear. After cooking, transfer the chicken to a serving pan and serve.

One-Dish Chicken & Rice

PREP TIME: 10 MINUTES • COOKING TIME: 40 MINUTES • TOTAL COOKING TIME: 50 MINUTES • SERVES: 4

Ingredients

1 cup long-grain white rice
1 cup cut frozen green beans
1 tablespoon minced fresh ginger
3 cloves garlic, minced
1 tablespoon toasted sesame oil
1 teaspoon kosher salt
1 teaspoon black pepper

1pound chicken wings

Direction:

1 In a 6-by-3-inch round heatproof pan, rice, green beans, ginger, garlic, sesame oil, salt, and pepper are mixed together. Stir to mix. Place chicken wings on top of the rice mixture. Wrap the pan in aluminum foil. Create a long slit in the foil to allow steam to escape the pan.

2 Place the pan in the basket of the air fryer. Set the air fryer to 375 degrees Fahrenheit for 30 minutes. Take off the foil. Adjust the Salter air fryer temperature to 400 degrees Fahrenheit for ten minutes, or until the chicken wings are fried and the oil has rendered into the rice and veggies, rotating the wings midway through cooking.

Lebanese Turkey Burgers with Feta & Tzatziki

PREP TIME: 25 MINUTES • COOKING TIME: 12 MINUTES • TOTAL COOKING TIME: 37 MINUTES • SERVES: 4

Ingredients

1 small yellow onion, finely diced
1 clove garlic, minced
2 tablespoons chopped fresh parsley
2 teaspoons Lebanese Seven-Spice Mix
½ teaspoon kosher salt
1 large cucumber, peeled and grated
2 to 3 cloves garlic, minced
1 cup plain Greek yogurt
1 tablespoon tahini (sesame paste)
1 tablespoon fresh lemon juice
½ teaspoon kosher salt
Vegetable oil spray
For Serving
4 lettuce leaves or 2 whole-wheat pita breads, halved
8 slices ripe tomato
1 cup baby spinach
⅓ cup crumbled feta cheese
1 pound ground turkey, chicken, or lamb

Direction:

1 *In a medium bowl, thoroughly combine all of the tzatziki ingredients. Cover and refrigerate until serving.*

2 *In a large bowl, combine the ground turkey, onion, garlic, parsley, spice blend, and salt for the burgers. Mix gradually until thoroughly combined. The turkey should be divided into four pieces and formed into round patties.*

3 *Spray the basket of the Salter air fryer with vegetable oil spray. Place the patties in the air fryer basket in a single layer. 12 minutes at 400 degrees Fahrenheit and 400 degrees Fahrenheit. Each burger should be wrapped in a lettuce leaf or pita half. Include two tomato slices, spinach, cheese, and tzatziki in the sandwich.*

Sweet And Sour Chicken

PREP TIME: 5 MINUTES • COOKING TIME: 20 MINUTES • TOTAL COOKING TIME: 25 MINUTES • SERVES: 6

Ingredients

1/4 cup Soy sauce
3 Chicken Breasts, cubed
1/2 Cup Flour
1/2 Cup Cornstarch
2 Red Peppers, sliced
1Onion,chopped
2 Carrots, julienned
3/4 Cup Sugar
2 Tbsps Cornstarch
1/3 Cup Vinegar
2/3 Cup Water
1 Tbsp Ketchup

Direction:

1. The air fryer should be heated to 375 degrees Fahrenheit.
2. Shake the chicken, flour, and cornstarch in an airtight container to mix. Remove the chicken from the container and dispose of the remaining flour.
3. Cook the chicken in the Air Fryer for twenty minutes.
4. In a saucepan, combine sugar, water, vinegar, soy sauce, and ketchup using a whisk. Bring to a boil over medium heat before reducing the heat and simmering for two minutes. After cooking the chicken for 20 minutes in the Air fryer, add the vegetables and sauce mixture and cook for an additional 5 minutes. Serve over hot rice.

Easy Lemon Chicken Thighs

PREP TIME: 5 MINUTES • COOKING TIME: 10 MINUTES • TOTAL COOKING TIME: 15 MINUTES • SERVES: 4

Ingredients

1 teaspoon freshly ground black pepper
2 tablespoons olive oil
2 tablespoons Italian seasoning
2 tablespoons freshly squeezed lemon juice
1 teaspoon salt
1 lemon, sliced

Direction:

1. Salt and pepper the chicken thighs, then place them in a medium mixing basin. Toss the

chicken thighs with the olive oil, Italian seasoning, and lemon juice until they are well coated with oil. Add the wedges of lemon. Place the chicken thighs in a single layer in the basket of the Salter air fryer.

2 Set the Salter AF's temperature to 350 degrees Fahrenheit. Set the timer for 10 minutes and cook the food. Use tongs to turn the chicken. Reset the timer and cook for an additional 10 minutes. Confirm that the interior temperature of the chicken has reached 165 degrees Fahrenheit. Add cooking time as necessary. When the chicken is thoroughly done, plate it, serve it, and savor it.

Air Fryer Southern Fried Chicken

PREP TIME:15 MINUTES
·COOKING TIME: 26 MINUTES ·TOTAL COOKING TIME:1 HOUR 36 MINUTES·SERVES: 4
Ingredients

2 teaspoons garlic powder
½ cup buttermilk
2 teaspoons salt, plus 1 tablespoon
1 teaspoon freshly ground black pepper
1 pound chicken thighs and drumsticks
1 cup all-purpose flour
2 teaspoons onion powder
½ teaspoon sweet paprika

Direction:

1 In a large mixing basin, whisk together the buttermilk, 2 tablespoons of salt, and pepper. Add the chicken pieces to the bowl, and marinate them in the refrigerator for at least one hour, covered. Before the chicken has marinated for five minutes, prepare the dredging mixture. In a large mixing bowl, combine the flour, 1 tablespoon of salt, onion powder, garlic powder, and paprika. Spray the basket of the Salter air fryer with olive oil. Remove the chicken from the buttermilk mixture and coat it with flour. Remove any surplus flour. Place the chicken pieces in a single layer in the greased Salter air fryer basket, leaving space between each piece. Olive oil is liberally sprayed onto the bird.

2 Set the Salter AF's temperature to 390 degrees Fahrenheit. Cook the dish for 13 minutes after setting the timer for 13 minutes. Use tongs to rotate the chicken. Spray liberally with olive oil. Reset the timer and cook for a further 13 minutes. Confirm that the interior temperature of the chicken has reached 165 degrees Fahrenheit. Adapt the cooking time accordingly. When the chicken is thoroughly done, plate it, serve it, and savor it!

Buffalo Chicken Wings

PREP TIME: 5 MINUTES · COOKING TIME: 30 MINUTES
· TOTAL COOKING TIME: 35 MINUTES · SERVES: 8
Ingredients

1-2 tbsp. brown sugar

1 tbsp. Worcestershire sauce
½ C. vegan butter
½ C. cayenne pepper sauce
1 tsp. salt
4 pounds chicken wings

Direction:

1 With a whisk, salt, brown sugar, Worcestershire sauce, butter, and hot sauce are blended and set aside. Dry wings and place in an air fryer.
2 Set temperature to 380 degrees Fahrenheit and timer to 25 minutes. Cook halfway through by tossing. When the timer goes off, shake the wings and increase the temperature to 400 degrees for an additional 5 minutes.
3 Remove the wings and set them in a large basin. Add sauce and mix thoroughly.
4 Serve alongside celery sticks.

Perfect Chicken Parmesan

PREP TIME: 5 MINUTES • COOKING TIME: 25 MINUTES • TOTAL COOKING TIME: 30 MINUTES • SERVES: 2

Ingredients

1 cup of breadcrumbs
2 medium-sized eggs
Pinch of salt and pepper
1 tablespoon of dried oregano
1 cup of marinara sauce
2 slices of provolone cheese
2 large white meat chicken breasts
1 tablespoon of parmesan cheese

Direction:

1 Cover the Air fryer's basket with aluminum foil, leaving the edges free for air circulation.
2 The air fryer should be preheated to 350 degrees Fahrenheit. In a mixing bowl, beat the eggs until they are frothy and the yolks and whites are thoroughly blended, then set aside.
3 Separately, combine the breadcrumbs, oregano, salt, and pepper in a basin and set aside. Coat the raw chicken breasts on both sides with the dry ingredients, one at a time, before immersing them in the wet components and then dipping them back into the dry ingredients. This double coating will ensure an air-fried dish that is crispier and more flavorful.
4 Place the breaded chicken breasts in a single layer on the foil covering the Air fryer basket.
5 Set the Salter air fryer's timer to 10 minutes.
6 After ten minutes, the air fryer will shut off, and the chicken should be halfway done with a crust that is beginning to brown.
7 Flip each piece of chicken with tongs to achieve even cooking.
8 Reset the air fryer to 320 degrees for a further 10 minutes.

9 In a 7-inch heat-safe skillet, pour half of the marinara sauce while the chicken is cooking.
10 When the air fryer shuts off after 15 minutes, remove the chicken breasts with tongs and place them in the pan with marinara. Drizzle the remaining marinara sauce over the fried chicken, add the provolone cheese slices on top, and then sprinkle the parmesan cheese over the entire dish.
11 Reset the temperature for five minutes to 350 degrees.
12 Using tongs or oven mitts, remove the dish from the air fryer when it shuts off after 5 minutes. The chicken will be adequately fried and the cheese will be melted and subtly browned. Serve when still hot!

Air Fryer Grilled Chicken Breasts

PREP TIME: 5 MINUTES • COOKING TIME: 14 MINUTES • TOTAL COOKING TIME: 19 MINUTES • SERVES: 4

Ingredients

1 teaspoon salt
½ teaspoon freshly ground black pepper
1 teaspoon dried parsley
2 tablespoons olive oil, divided
½ teaspoon garlic powder
3 boneless, skinless chicken breasts

Direction:

1 Combine the garlic powder, salt, pepper, and chopped parsley in a small bowl. Rub each chicken breast with one tablespoon of olive oil and one-half of the seasoning blend. Place the chicken breast in the air fryer's basket.
2 Adjust the temperature of the Salter AF to 370 degrees Fahrenheit. Set the grill timer for 7 minutes.
3 Using tongs, turn the chicken and coat it with the remaining olive oil and seasonings. Reset the timer and grill for an additional 7 minutes. Confirm that the interior temperature of the chicken has reached 165 degrees Fahrenheit. Adapt the cooking time accordingly.
4 After cooking, transfer the chicken to a serving pan and serve.

Zingy & Nutty Chicken Wings

PREP TIME: 5 MINUTES • COOKING TIME: 18 MINUTES • TOTAL COOKING TIME: 23 MINUTES • SERVES: 4

Ingredients

1 tablespoon fish sauce
1 tablespoon fresh lemon juice
1 teaspoon sugar
12 chicken middle wings, cut into half
2 fresh lemongrass stalks, chopped finely

¼ cup unsalted cashews, crushed

Direction:

1. In a bowl, combine fish sauce, lime juice, and sugar.
2. Add wings to the mixture and liberally coat them. Refrigerate for approximately 1 to 2 hours to marinate.
3. Preheat the air fryer to 355 degrees Fahrenheit.
4. In the pan of the Air fryer, place lemongrass stalks. Cook for roughly 2 to 3 minutes. Take the cashew mixture out of the Air fryer and place it in a bowl. Set the air fryer's temperature to 390 degrees Fahrenheit.
5. Insert the chicken wings into the Air fryer. Cook for an another 13 to 15 minutes.
6. Transfer the wings to serving plates. Serve garnished with cashew mixture.

Pesto-Cream Chicken with Cherry Tomatoes

PREP TIME: 10 MINUTES • COOKING TIME: 15 MINUTES • TOTAL COOKING TIME: 25 MINUTES • SERVES: 4

Ingredients

Vegetable oil spray
½ cup prepared pesto
¼ cup half-and-half
¼ grated Parmesan cheese
½ to 1 teaspoon red pepper flakes
1 pound boneless, skinless chicken thighs, halved crosswise
1 small onion, sliced
½cup sliced red and/or green bell peppers
½ cup halved cherry tomatoes

Direction:

1. Prepare a 6-by-3-inch round pan with cooking spray containing vegetable oil and set aside. In a large bowl, combine pesto, half-and-half, cheese, and red pepper flakes. Whisk until thoroughly mixed. Add the chicken and coat with the sauce. Transfer the sauce and chicken to the pan that has been prepared. The onion, bell pepper, and tomatoes should be scattered on top.
2. Place the pan in the basket of the air fryer. 15 minutes at 350 degrees Fahrenheit and 350 degrees Fahrenheit. Ensure the chicken has reached an internal temperature of 165°F by using a meat thermometer.

Peanut Chicken

PREP TIME: 15 MINUTES • COOKING TIME: 20 MINUTES • TOTAL COOKING TIME: 1 HOUR 5 MINUTES • SERVES: 4

Ingredients

¼ cup chopped green onions, for garnish

¼ cup creamy peanut butter
2 tablespoons sweet chili sauce
2 tablespoons fresh lime juice
1 tablespoon sriracha
1 tablespoon soy sauce
1 teaspoon minced fresh ginger
1 clove garlic, minced
½ teaspoon kosher salt
½ cup hot water
1 pound bone-in chicken thighs
2 tablespoons chopped fresh cilantro, for garnish
2 to 3 tablespoons crushed roasted and salted peanuts, for garnish

Direction:

1. In a small bowl, combine peanut butter, sweet chili sauce, lime juice, sriracha, soy sauce, ginger, garlic, and salt. Whisk in the heated water until a smooth consistency is achieved. Pour half of the sauce over the chicken in a resealable plastic bag. Save any leftover sauce for dishing. Seal the bag and massage the chicken until it is evenly coated. Marinate for 30 minutes at room temperature or up to 24 hours in the refrigerator. Take the chicken out of the bag and dispose of the marinade. Place the chicken in the air fryer's basket.
2. Set the air fryer to 350 degrees Fahrenheit for 20 minutes. Ensure the chicken has reached an internal temperature of 165°F by using a meat thermometer. Transfer the chicken to a serving dish. Toss with peanuts, cilantro, and green onions. Serve with the sauce that was set aside for dipping.

Basil-Garlic Breaded Chicken Bake

PREP TIME: 5 MINUTES • COOKING TIME: 25 MINUTES • TOTAL COOKING TIME: 30 MINUTES • SERVES: 2

Ingredients

1/4 cup dry bread crumbs
2 boneless skinless chicken breast halves
1 tablespoon butter, melted
1 large tomato, seeded and chopped
2 garlic cloves, minced
1 1/2 tablespoons minced fresh basil
1/2 tablespoon olive oil
1/2 teaspoon salt
1/4 cup all-purpose flour
1/4 cup egg substitute
1/4 cup grated Parmesan cheese
1/4 teaspoon pepper

Direction:

1. In a small dish, whisk egg substitute, and place flour in a separate bowl. Coat chicken with flour, followed by egg, and finally flour. In a small bowl, mix butter, breadcrumbs, and cheese completely. Sprinkle over chicken. Spray the air fryer's baking pan lightly with cooking spray. Place breaded chicken in the pan's bottom. Wrap with foil.
2. For 20 minutes, cook at 390 degrees Fahrenheit.
3. Meanwhile, thoroughly mix the remaining ingredient in a bowl. Remove the foil from the pan and then pour the other ingredients over the chicken. Prepare for 8 minutes. Serve with pleasure.

PORK RECIPES

Pork Taquitos

PREP TIME: 10 MINUTES • COOKING TIME: 16 MINUTES • TOTAL COOKING TIME: 26 MINUTES • SERVES: 8

Ingredients

1 juiced lime
10 whole wheat tortillas
2 ½ C. shredded mozzarella cheese
30 ounces of cooked and shredded pork tenderloin

Direction:

1 Ensure the air fryer is preheated to 380 degrees.
2 Combine meat and lime juice with care.
3 Soften tortillas in the microwave using a moistened paper towel.
4 Add approximately 3 ounces of pork and 1/4 cup of cheese to each tortilla. Compactly roll them up.
5 The basket of the Salter air fryer is sprayed with olive oil.
6 Temperature and timer are set to 380 degrees Fahrenheit and 10 minutes, respectively. Air-fry taquitos for 7 to 10 minutes, or until the tortillas acquire a light golden hue, being sure to flip them halfway through the process.

Cajun Bacon Pork Loin Fillet

PREP TIME: 10 •COOKING TIME: 20 MINUTES •TOTAL COOKING TIME:1 HOUR 30MINUTES•SERVES: 6

Ingredients

6 slices bacon
1½ pounds pork loin fillet or pork tenderloin
3 tablespoons olive oil
2 tablespoons Cajun Spice Mix
Salt
Olive oil spray

Direction:

1 In order for the pork to fit in the air fryer basket, it must be halved.
2 Place the two meat portions in a resealable plastic bag. If using, add the oil, Cajun seasoning, and salt to taste. Seal the bag and knead the meat to evenly distribute the oil and spices. Marinate for at least one hour and up to twenty-four hours in the refrigerator.

3 Remove the pork from the bag and wrap each piece with three bacon pieces. Spray the basket of the Salter air fryer with olive oil spray. Insert the meat into an air fryer. Set the air fryer to 350 degrees Fahrenheit for 15 minutes. Increase the temperature to 400 degrees Fahrenheit for five minutes. Using a meat thermometer, verify that the internal temperature of the meat has reached 145 degrees Fahrenheit.
4 The meat should rest for 10 minutes. Slice into six medallions and serve.

Panko-Breaded Pork Chops

PREP TIME: 5 MINUTES • COOKING TIME: 12 MINUTES • TOTAL COOKING TIME: 17 MINUTES • SERVES: 6

Ingredients

5 (3½- to 5-ounce) pork chops (bone-in or boneless)
Seasoning salt
Pepper
¼ cup all-purpose flour
2 tablespoons panko bread crumbs
Cooking oil

Direction:

1 The pork chops are seasoned with salt and pepper to taste.
2 Coat the pork chops on both sides with flour, and then with panko bread crumbs.
3 The pork chops should be placed in the air fryer. Stacking them is OK.
4 The pork chops are sprayed with frying oil. Prepare for six minutes.
5 Activate the Air fryer and turn the pork chops over. Continue cooking for six minutes
6 Before serving, chill.
7 Generally speaking, bone-in pork chops are more juicy than boneless. If you love pork chops that are exceptionally juicy, get those with the bone in.

Porchetta-Style Pork Chops

PREP TIME: 10 MINUTES • COOKING TIME: 15 MINUTES • TOTAL COOKING TIME: 25 MINUTES • SERVES: 2

Ingredients

1 tablespoon extra-virgin olive oil
Grated zest of 1 lemon
2 cloves garlic, minced
2 teaspoons chopped fresh rosemary
1 teaspoon finely chopped fresh sage
1 teaspoon fennel seeds, lightly crushed
¼ to ½ teaspoon red pepper flakes
1 teaspoon kosher salt
1 teaspoon black pepper
(8-ounce) center-cut bone-in pork chops, about 1 inch thick

Direction:

1. In a small bowl, mix together the olive oil, citrus zest, garlic, rosemary, sage, fennel seeds, red pepper, salt, and black pepper. Stir until a paste is formed, mashing the herbs with the back of a spoon. On all sides of the pork chops, the seasoning combination was applied.
2. Place the chops in the basket of an air fryer. Set the air fryer to 375 degrees Fahrenheit for 15 minutes. Using a meat thermometer, verify that the chops have reached an internal temperature of 145 degrees Fahrenheit.

Apricot Glazed Pork Tenderloins

PREP TIME: 5 MINUTES • COOKING TIME: 30 MINUTES • TOTAL COOKING TIME: 35 MINUTES • SERVES: 3

Ingredients

1 teaspoon salt
1/2 teaspoon pepper
1-lb pork tenderloin
2 tablespoons minced fresh rosemary or 1 tablespoon dried rosemary, crushed
2 tablespoons olive oil, divided
1 garlic cloves, minced
Apricot Glaze Ingredients
1 cup apricot preserves
3 garlic cloves, minced
4 tablespoons lemon juice

Direction:

1. In a bowl, combine pepper, salt, garlic, oil, and rosemary. Brush pork well. If necessary, cut pork in half lengthwise to fit in an air fryer. Spray the baking pan of the air fryer lightly with cooking spray. Add pork.
2. In an air fryer preheated to 390 °F, sear pork for 3 minutes per side.
3. In the meantime, combine glaze ingredients in a small basin. The pork should be basted every 5 minutes. Cook for 20 minutes at 330 degrees Fahrenheit. Serve with pleasure.

Sweet & Spicy Country-Style Ribs

PREP TIME: 10 MINUTES • COOKING TIME: 25 MINUTES • TOTAL COOKING TIME: 35 MINUTES • SERVES: 4

Ingredients

2 tablespoons smoked paprika
1 teaspoon garlic powder
1 teaspoon onion powder
1 teaspoon dry mustard
1 teaspoon ground cumin

1 teaspoon kosher salt
1 teaspoon black pepper
¼ to ½ teaspoon cayenne pepper
1½ pounds boneless country-style pork ribs
2 tablespoons brown sugar
1 cup barbecue sauce

Direction:

1 In a small bowl, combine the brown sugar, paprika, garlic powder, onion powder, dry mustard, cumin, black pepper, and cayenne. Combine until fully blended.
2 To dry the ribs, use a paper towel. Liberally sprinkle the rub on both sides of the ribs and work it into the meat with your fingertips.
3 Place the ribs in the basket of the air fryer. Set the air fryer to 350 degrees Fahrenheit for 15 minutes. Brush the ribs with half a cup of barbecue sauce and turn them over. Continue cooking for 10 minutes more. Verify that the pork has attained an internal temperature of 145°F using a meat thermometer. Serve with any leftover barbecue sauce.

Pork Tenders With Bell Peppers

PREP TIME: 5 MINUTES • COOKING TIME: 15 MINUTES • TOTAL COOKING TIME: 20 MINUTES • SERVES: 4

Ingredients

1 Bell Pepper, in thin strips
1 Red Onion, sliced
2 Tsps Provencal Herbs
Black Pepper to taste
1 Tbsp Olive Oil
11 Ozs Pork Tenderloin
1/2 Tbsp Mustard

Direction:

1 The air fryer should be heated to 390 degrees Celsius.
2 Combine the bell pepper strips, onion, herbs, and a touch of salt and pepper in a baking dish.
3 It is necessary to add a half teaspoon of olive oil to the mixture.
4 Rub the pork tenderloin with a mixture of salt, pepper, and mustard.
5 Coat the pieces with the remaining olive oil and set them upright on the pepper mixture in the baking dish.
6 Insert the dish into the Air fryer. Set a 15-minute timer and roast the meat and vegetables.
7 Turn the meat and incorporate the peppers about the midpoint of cooking.
8 Complement with a fresh salad

Wonton Meatballs

PREP TIME: 15 MINUTES • COOKING TIME: 10 MINUTES • TOTAL COOKING TIME: 25 MINUTES • SERVES: 4

Ingredients

¼ cup chopped fresh cilantro or parsley
1 tablespoon minced fresh ginger
3 cloves garlic, minced
2 teaspoons soy sauce
1 teaspoon oyster sauce
½ teaspoon kosher salt
1 pound ground pork
2 large eggs
¼ cup chopped green onions (white and green parts)
1 teaspoon black pepper

Direction:

1 In the paddle attachment of a stand mixer, combine pork, eggs, green onions, cilantro, ginger, garlic, soy sauce, oyster sauce, salt, and pepper. Mix on low speed for two to three minutes, or until all ingredients are combined.
2 Form the mixture into 12 meatballs and place them in the air fryer basket in a single layer.
3 Ten minutes at 350 degrees Fahrenheit and 350 degrees Fahrenheit. Using a meat thermometer, verify that the meatballs have reached an internal temperature of 145 degrees Fahrenheit.
4 Serve the meatballs by placing them in a serving bowl.

Barbecue Flavored Pork Ribs

PREP TIME: 5 MINUTES • COOKING TIME: 15 MINUTES • TOTAL COOKING TIME: 25 MINUTES • SERVES: 6

Ingredients

¼ cup honey, divided
¾ cup BBQ sauce
2 tablespoons tomato ketchup
1 tablespoon Worcestershire sauce
1 tablespoon soy sauce
½ teaspoon garlic powder
Freshly ground white pepper, to taste
1¾ pound pork ribs

Direction:

1. Except for the pork ribs, combine three tablespoons of honey with the remaining ingredients in a large basin. Marinate for roughly 20 minutes in the refrigerator. Preheat the air fryer to 355 degrees Fahrenheit. Place the ribs in the basket of an Air fryer.
2. Prepare food for 13 minutes. Coat the ribs with the leftover honey after removing

them from the Air fryer. Serve warm.

Easy Air Fryer Marinated Pork Tenderloin

PREP TIME:10 MINUTES •COOKING TIME:30 MINUTES •TOTAL COOKING TIME:1 HOUR 40 MINUTES•SERVES:4-6

Ingredients

½ teaspoon freshly ground black pepper
¼ cup olive oil
¼ cup soy sauce
¼ cup freshly squeezed lemon juice
1 garlic clove, minced
1 tablespoon Dijon mustard
1 teaspoon salt
2 pounds pork tenderloin

Direction:

1. In a large bowl, mix the marinade ingredients. In a bowl, whisk together the olive oil, soy sauce, lemon juice, garlic, Dijon mustard, salt, and pepper. Set aside 1/4 cup marinade.
2. Pour the remaining marinade over the tenderloin in a large basin. Cover and refrigerate for approximately one hour. Place the pork tenderloin that has been marinated in the air fryer basket.
3. Set the Salter AF's temperature to 400 degrees Fahrenheit. Set the timer for 10 minutes and roast the meat. Using tongs, flip the pig and baste it with half of the leftover marinade. Reset the timer and roast for a further 10 minutes. Flip the pork using tongs, then baste with the remaining marinade. Reset the timer and continue roasting for an additional 10 minutes, for a total of 30 minutes.

Balsamic Glazed Pork Chops

PREP TIME: 5 MINUTES • COOKING TIME: 50 MINUTES • TOTAL COOKING TIME: 55 MINUTES • SERVES: 4

Ingredients

¾ cup balsamic vinegar
1 ½ tablespoons sugar
1 tablespoon butter
3 tablespoons olive oil
3 tablespoons salt
3 pork rib chops

Direction:

1. Place all ingredients in a bowl and marinate the meat for at least two hours in the refrigerator. The air fryer should be preheated to 390 degrees Fahrenheit. Insert the grill pan accessory into the air fryer.
2. For even grilling, grill the pork chops for 20 minutes, turning the meat every 10 minutes. Pour

the balsamic vinegar into a saucepan and cook for at least 10 minutes, or until the sauce has thickened. Before serving, glaze the meat with the sauce.

Perfect Air Fried Pork Chops

PREP TIME: 5 MINUTES • COOKING TIME: 17 MINUTES • TOTAL COOKING TIME: 22 MINUTES • SERVES: 4

Ingredients

3 cups bread crumbs
½ cup grated Parmesan cheese
2 tablespoons vegetable oil
2 teaspoons salt
2 teaspoons sweet paprika
½ teaspoon onion powder
¼ teaspoon garlic powder
6 (½-inch-thick) bone-in pork chops

Direction:

1 Spray the basket of the Salter air fryer with olive oil. In a large resealable bag, combine the bread crumbs, Parmesan cheese, oil, salt, paprika, onion powder, and garlic powder. Seal the bag and shake it a few times in order for the spices to combine together. One by one, place the pork chops in the bag and shake to coat.

2 Place the pork chops in a single layer in the oiled Salter air fryer basket. Carefully avoid overfilling the basket. Spray the pork chops with olive oil liberally to prevent raw, powdery breading. Adjust the temperature of the Salter AF to 360 degrees Fahrenheit. Set the timer for 10 minutes and roast the meat. Use tongs to turn the chops. Spray them with olive oil liberally. Reset the timer and cook for a further 7 minutes. Ensure the internal temperature of the pork has reached 145 degrees Fahrenheit. Adapt the cooking time accordingly.

Rustic Pork Ribs

PREP TIME: 5 MINUTES • COOKING TIME: 15 MINUTES • TOTAL COOKING TIME: 25 MINUTES • SERVES: 4

Ingredients

1 tablespoon cornstarch
1 rack of pork ribs
3 tablespoons dry red wine
1 tablespoon soy sauce
1/2 teaspoon dried thyme
1/2 teaspoon onion powder
1/2 teaspoon garlic powder
1/2 teaspoon ground black pepper
1 teaspoon smoke salt
1/2 teaspoon olive oil

Direction:

1. The fryer should be preheated to 390 degrees Fahrenheit. Put all of the ingredients in a bowl and let them marinade for at least one hour.
2. Cook the marinated ribs at 390 degrees Fahrenheit for 25 minutes. Serve warm.

Air Fryer Baby Back Ribs

PREP TIME: 5 MINUTES • COOKING TIME: 25 MINUTES • TOTAL COOKING TIME: 30 MINUTES • SERVES: 4

Ingredients

1 rack baby back ribs
1 tablespoon garlic powder
1 teaspoon freshly ground black pepper
2 tablespoons salt
1 cup barbecue sauce (any type)

Direction:

1. A paper towel is used to dry the ribs.
2. The ribs are seasoned with garlic powder, pepper, and salt.
3. Seasoned ribs should be placed in the air fryer.
4. Set the Salter AF's temperature to 400 degrees Fahrenheit. Set the grill timer for 10 minutes.
5. Using tongs, turn the ribs over.
6. Reset the timer and continue grilling for 10 minutes.
7. Using a pastry brush, spread barbecue sauce to the ribs, then set a timer for 3 to 5 minutes and grill the ribs.

Keto Parmesan Crusted Pork Chops

PREP TIME: 10 MINUTES • COOKING TIME: 15 MINUTES • TOTAL COOKING TIME: 25 MINUTES • SERVES: 8

Ingredients

½ tsp. salt
3 tbsp. grated parmesan cheese
1 C. pork rind crumbs
2 beaten eggs
¼ tsp. chili powder
½ tsp. onion powder
1 tsp. smoked paprika
¼ tsp. pepper
4-6 thick boneless pork chops

Direction:

1 Ensure your air fryer has been preheated to 400 degrees F.
2 The pork chops should be seasoned on both sides with pepper and salt.
3 Pulse pig rinds in a food processor into crumbs. Mix together breadcrumbs and spices. Add beaten eggs to another bowl.
4 Dip pork chops into eggs then into pork rind crumb mixture.
5 Spray pork chops with olive oil and place them in the basket of an air fryer. Set temperature to 400 degrees Fahrenheit and timer to 15 minutes.

Pork Milanese

PREP TIME: 10 MINUTES • COOKING TIME: 12 MINUTES • TOTAL COOKING TIME: 22 MINUTES • SERVES: 4

Ingredients

4 (1-inch) boneless pork chops
Fine sea salt and ground black pepper
2 large eggs
¾ cup powdered Parmesan cheese about 2¼ ounces
Chopped fresh parsley, for garnish
Lemon slices, for serving

Direction:

1 Spray avocado oil on the Salter air fryer basket. Adjust the temperature of the Salter air fryer to 400 degrees Fahrenheit. Place the pork chops between two sheets of plastic wrap and pound them to a thickness of 14 inches using the flat side of a meat tenderizer. Season the chops with salt and pepper on both sides. Lightly beat the eggs in a small basin. Equally divide the Parmesan cheese between two bowls and arrange the bowls in this order: Parmesan, eggs, Parmesan. Coat a pork chop thoroughly on both sides and all corners by dredging it in the Parmesan, dipping it in the eggs, and then dredging it once more in the Parmesan. Continue with remaining chops.
2 Place the chops in the basket of the Salter air fryer and cook for 12 minutes, or until the internal temperature reaches 145 degrees Fahrenheit, rotating the chops halfway through.
3 Garnish with fresh parsley and serve with lemon slices immediately. Refrigerate leftovers for up to three days in an airtight container. Reheat in a preheated air fryer at 390°F for 5 minutes, or until thoroughly heated.

Crispy Fried Pork Chops the Southern Way

PREP TIME: 10 MINUTES • COOKING TIME: 25 MINUTES • TOTAL COOKING TIME: 35 MINUTES • SERVES: 4

Ingredients

½ cup low fat buttermilk
½ teaspoon black pepper
½ teaspoon Tabasco sauce

teaspoon paprika
½ cup all-purpose flour
3 bone-in pork chops

Direction:

1 In a Ziploc bag, combine the pork chops, buttermilk, and spicy sauce. Allow to marinate in the refrigerator for at least one hour.
2 In a bowl, combine the flour, paprika, and black pepper.
3 Take the pork out of the Ziploc bag and dredge it in the flour mixture.
4 The air fryer should be preheated to 390 degrees Fahrenheit.
5 The pork chops are sprayed with frying oil.
6 Place in the basket of the Salter air fryer and cook for 25 minutes.

Italian Sausages with Peppers and Onions

PREP TIME: 5 MINUTES • COOKING TIME: 28 MINUTES • TOTAL COOKING TIME: 33 MINUTES • SERVES: 3

Ingredients

1 medium onion, thinly sliced
1 yellow or orange bell pepper, thinly sliced
1 red bell pepper, thinly sliced
¼ cup avocado oil or melted coconut oil
1 teaspoon fine sea salt
6 Italian sausages
Dijon mustard, for serving (optional)

Direction:

1 Adjust the temperature of the Salter air fryer to 400 degrees Fahrenheit. In a big bowl, the onion and peppers should be placed. Drizzle the oil over the vegetables and toss to evenly coat them. Season the dish with salt.
2 In a 6-inch pie pan, place the onion and peppers and cook them in an air fryer for 8 minutes, stirring halfway through. Take the food out of the air fryer and set aside.
3 Spray avocado oil on the Salter air fryer basket. Place the sausages in the basket of the Salter air fryer and cook for 20 minutes, or until golden and crisp. During the last minute or two of cooking, add the onion and peppers to the sausage basket to fully warm them.
4 Place the onion and peppers on a serving plate, then lay the sausages on top. If desired, mustard should be served on the side.
5 Refrigerate leftovers in an airtight jar for up to seven days or freeze them for up to one month. Reheat in a preheated air fryer at 390°F for three minutes, or until thoroughly heated.

Fried Pork Quesadilla

PREP TIME: 10 MINUTES • COOKING TIME: 12 MINUTES • TOTAL COOKING TIME: 22 MINUTES • SERVES: 2

Ingredients

¼ cup of shredded pepper-jack cheese
Two 6-inch corn or flour tortilla shells
1 medium-sized pork shoulder, approximately 4 ounces, sliced
½ medium-sized white onion, sliced
½ medium-sized red pepper, sliced
½ medium sized green pepper, sliced
½ medium sized yellow pepper, sliced
¼ cup of shredded mozzarella cheese

Direction:

1 The air fryer should be preheated to 350 degrees Fahrenheit.
2 Allowing the fluids from the pork and veggies to mingle, grill the pork, onion, and peppers wrapped in foil for 20 minutes at high heat in the same pan. Remove the foil-wrapped pork and veggies from the oven. While they are cooling, sprinkle half of the shredded cheese over one of the tortillas, followed by the pork, onions, and peppers, and finally the remaining cheese. Add the second tortilla on top. Place immediately on the hot surface of the basket of the Air fryer.
3 Set the timer on the Salter air fryer to six minutes. When the Air fryer goes off after 6 minutes, flip the tortillas with a spatula; the cheese should be sufficiently melted so it won't break apart, but be cautious not to spill the toppings!
4 Adjust the temperature to 350 degrees for a further six minutes.
5 After six minutes, the tortillas should be browned and crisp, and the pork, onion, peppers, and cheese should be crisp, hot, and delectable. Remove with tongs and allow to cool for a few minutes on a serving plate before slicing.

Cilantro-Mint Pork BBQ Thai Style

PREP TIME: 5 MINUTES • COOKING TIME: 15 MINUTES • TOTAL COOKING TIME: 20 MINUTES • SERVES: 3

Ingredients

3 tablespoons chopped mint
1 minced hot chile
1 minced shallot
1-pound ground pork
2 tablespoons fish sauce
2 tablespoons lime juice
3 tablespoons basil
3 tablespoons cilantro

Direction:

1 By hand, properly combine all Ingredients in a shallow basin. Create one-inch-wide ovals.

Insert ovals onto skewers. Place on the air fryer's skewer rack.

2 For 15 minutes, cook at 360 degrees Fahrenheit. Halfway through the cooking process, rotate the skewers. When necessary, cook in batches. Serve with enthusiasm.

Pork Wonton Wonderful

PREP TIME: 10 MINUTES • COOKING TIME: 25 MINUTES • TOTAL COOKING TIME: 35 MINUTES • SERVES: 3

Ingredients

8 wanton wrappers
4 ounces of raw minced pork
1 medium-sized green apple
1 cup of water, for wetting the wanton wrappers
1 tablespoon of vegetable oil
½ tablespoon of oyster sauce
1 tablespoon of soy sauce
Large pinch of ground white pepper

Direction:

1 Cover the Air fryer's basket with aluminum foil, leaving the edges free for air circulation. The air fryer should be preheated to 350 degrees Fahrenheit. In a small mixing bowl, combine the oyster sauce, soy sauce, and white pepper, and then stir in the ground pork. Cover and marinate for at least 15 minutes in the refrigerator. Core the apple and cut it into cubes that are smaller than bite-sized. Add the apples to the beef mixture that is marinating and thoroughly blend. Spread the filling on the wonton wrappers, then fill each with a heaping spoonful. Wrap the wontons in triangles, ensuring that the wrappers completely encase the filling, and seal with a drop of water. Coat each filled and encased wonton generously with vegetable oil in order to get a fantastically crispy fry. Place the wontons in the air fryer's foil-lined basket.

2 Set the timer on the Salter air fryer to 25 minutes. Halfway through cooking, firmly shake the handle of the Salter air fryer basket to ensure even frying of the wontons. When the Air fryer goes off after 25 minutes, the wontons will be golden-brown and crunchy on the surface and juicy and flavorful on the inside. Serve immediately from the basket of the Salter air fryer and enjoy while still hot.

Crispy Roast Garlic-Salt Pork

PREP TIME: 5 MINUTES • COOKING TIME: 45 MINUTES • TOTAL COOKING TIME: 50 MINUTES • SERVES: 4

Ingredients

1 teaspoon Chinese five spice powder
1 teaspoon white pepper
2 pounds pork belly
2 teaspoons garlic salt

Direction:

1. The air fryer should be preheated to 390 degrees Fahrenheit.
2. Combine all the spices in a bowl to make the dry rub.
3. The skin of the pork belly should be scored with a knife, and the entire belly should be seasoned with the spice rub.
4. Cook for 40 to 45 minutes in the Salter air fryer basket until the skin is crispy.
5. Chop before serving.

Scotch Eggs

PREP TIME: 10 MINUTES • COOKING TIME: 15 MINUTES • TOTAL COOKING TIME: 25 MINUTES • SERVES: 8

Ingredients

2 pounds ground pork or ground beef
2 teaspoons fine sea salt
½ teaspoon ground black pepper, plus more for garnish
8 large hard-boiled eggs, peeled
2 cups pork dust
Dijon mustard, for serving (optional)

Direction:

1. Spray avocado oil on the Salter air fryer basket. Preheat the Salter air fryer to 400 degrees Fahrenheit. Place the ground pork in a large bowl, season with salt and pepper, and mix thoroughly with your hands. Place a peeled egg in the center of about a quarter-pound of ground pork that has been flattened in your palm. Completely wrap the pork around the egg. Continue with remaining eggs. Place the pork dust in a medium-sized bowl. Roll each egg covered in ground pork in the pork dust and make a crust by pressing the pork dust into the egg with your palms.
2. Place the eggs in the basket of the Salter air fryer and mist them with avocado oil.
3. Cook the eggs for 15 minutes, or until the pork reaches an internal temperature of 145 degrees Fahrenheit and the exterior is golden brown. If preferred, garnish with ground black pepper and serve with Dijon mustard.
4. Refrigerate leftovers in an airtight jar for up to seven days, or freeze them for up to one month. Reheat at 400 degrees Fahrenheit for three minutes in an air fryer that has been warmed.

Italian Parmesan Breaded Pork Chops

PREP TIME: 5 MINUTES • COOKING TIME: 25 MINUTES • TOTAL COOKING TIME: 30 MINUTES • SERVES: 5

Ingredients

5 (3½- to 5-ounce) pork chops (bone-in or boneless)
1 teaspoon Italian seasoning

Seasoning salt
Pepper
¼ cup all-purpose flour
2 tablespoons Italian bread crumbs
3 tablespoons finely grated Parmesan cheese
Cooking oil

Direction:

1. The pork chops are seasoned to taste with Italian seasoning, salt, and black pepper. Coat both sides of the pork chops with flour, then coat both sides with bread crumbs and Parmesan cheese.
2. The pork chops should be placed in the Air fryer. Stacking them is permitted. The pork chops are sprayed with frying oil. Prepare for six minutes. Activate the Air fryer and turn the pork chops over. Continue cooking for another 6 minutes. Before serving, chill. You can add more taste by substituting chicken or pork rub for seasoned salt. These rubs are available in the spice section of the shop.

Pork Tenderloin with Avocado Lime Sauce

PREP TIME:10 MINUTES ·COOKING TIME:15 MINUTES ·TOTAL COOKING TIME: 2 HOURS 25MINUTES· SERVES:4

Ingredients

Chopped fresh cilantro leaves, for garnish
Lime slices, for serving
MARINADE:
½ cup lime juice
Grated zest of 1 lime
2 teaspoons stevia glycerite, or ¼ teaspoon liquid stevia
3 cloves garlic, minced
1½ teaspoons fine sea salt
1 teaspoon chili powder, or more for more heat
1 teaspoon smoked paprika
1 medium-sized ripe avocado, roughly chopped
½ cup full-fat sour cream
Grated zest of 1 lime
Juice of 1 lime
2 cloves garlic, roughly chopped
Pico de gallo, for serving
½ teaspoon fine sea salt
¼ teaspoon ground black pepper
1 pound pork tenderloin

Direction:

1 In a casserole dish of medium size, properly combine all marinade ingredients. Add the tenderloin to the marinade and fully coat it with it. Cover and marinate in the refrigerator for two hours or overnight.

2 Spray avocado oil on the basket of the Salter air fryer. Preheat the Salter air fryer to 400 degrees Fahrenheit.

3 Take the pork out of the marinade and set it in the basket of an air fryer. 13 to 15 minutes, flipping after 7 minutes, or until the internal temperature of the pork reaches 145 degrees Fahrenheit. The pork should be transferred from the air fryer to a cutting board. Before slicing it into 12-inch-thick slices, allow it to rest for eight to ten minutes.

4 While the pork is cooking, prepare the sauce: Blend all the components for the sauce in a food processor until smooth. Taste the dish and adjust the seasoning as desired.

5 Place the pork pieces on a dish and drizzle the avocado lime sauce over them. Serve with lime slices and pico de gallo, then garnish with cilantro leaves.

6 Refrigerate leftovers for up to four days in an airtight container. Reheat in a preheated air fryer at 400°F for 5 minutes, or until thoroughly heated.

BEEF RECIPES

Cheeseburger Egg Rolls

PREP TIME: 10 MINUTES • COOKING TIME: 7 MINUTES • TOTAL COOKING TIME: 17 MINUTES • SERVES: 6

Ingredients

½ C. chopped onion
½ C. chopped bell pepper
¼ tsp. onion powder
¼ tsp. garlic powder
6 egg roll wrappers
6 chopped dill pickle chips
1 tbsp. yellow mustard
3 tbsp. cream cheese
3 tbsp. shredded cheddar cheese
8 ounces of raw lean ground beef

Direction:

1. Add meat, onion, and bell pepper to a skillet along with seasonings. Stir and shred the beef until it is fully cooked and the vegetables are tender. Remove the skillet from the heat and mix in the cream cheese, mustard, and cheddar cheese until melted. The beef mixture is poured into a bowl, then pickles are folded in.
2. Spread out egg wrappers and fill each with 1/6 of the meat mixture. Wet the edges of the egg roll wrapper with water. Fold the sides in toward the center and seal with water. Repeat with the remaining egg rolls.
3. Place rolls individually into the air fryer.
4. Set the temperature to 392 degrees Fahrenheit and the timer to seven minutes.

Air Fried Grilled Steak

PREP TIME: 5 MINUTES • COOKING TIME: 45 MINUTES • TOTAL COOKING TIME: 50 MINUTES • SERVES: 2

Ingredients

3 tablespoons butter, melted
3 tablespoons olive oil
2 top sirloin steaks
Salt and pepper to taste

Direction:

1 The Salter air fryer should be preheated for five minutes. Olive oil, salt, and pepper are used to season the sirloin steaks. Place the steak in the basket of an air fryer.
2 Cook at 350° for 45 minutes. When finished, serve with butter.

Beef Brisket Recipe from Texas

PREP TIME: 15 MINUTES • COOKING TIME: 1HOUR AND 30 MINUTES • SERVES: 8

Ingredients

1 bay leaf
1 tablespoon garlic powder
1 tablespoon onion powder
2 pounds beef brisket, trimmed
2 tablespoons chili powder
2 teaspoons dry mustard
4 tablespoons olive oil
1 ½ cup beef stock
Salt and pepper to taste

Direction:

1 The Salter air fryer should be preheated for five minutes. Place the ingredients in a deep baking dish that is suitable with an air fryer.
2 1 hour and 30 minutes at 400 degrees Fahrenheit.
3 Stir the meat every 30 minutes to help it absorb the sauce.

Savory Beefy Poppers

PREP TIME: 15 MINUTES • COOKING TIME: 15 MINUTES • TOTAL COOKING TIME: 30 MINUTES • SERVES: 8

Ingredients

8 medium jalapeño peppers, stemmed, halved, and seeded
1 (8-ounce) package cream cheese softened
2 pounds ground beef (85% lean)
1 teaspoon fine sea salt
½ teaspoon ground black pepper
8 slices thin-cut bacon
Fresh cilantro leaves, for garnish

Direction:

1 Spray avocado oil on the Salter air fryer basket. Adjust the temperature of the Salter air fryer to 400 degrees Fahrenheit. Each jalapeo half should be stuffed with a few teaspoons of cream cheese. Put the halves back together to create eight jalapeos.
2 Season the ground beef with salt and pepper, then combine with your hands. Place a stuffed

jalapeo in the center of a quarter-pound of ground beef that has been flattened in the palm of your hand. Fold the beef around the jalapeo to produce the shape of an egg. Wrap the beef-filled jalapeno in bacon and fasten it with a toothpick.

3 Place the jalapeos in the air fryer basket, leaving space between them. Cook for 15 minutes, or until the beef is fully cooked and the bacon is crunchy. Add cilantro as a garnish before serving. Refrigerate leftovers for three days in an airtight container or freeze them for up to one month. Reheat bacon in a preheated air fryer at 350 degrees Fahrenheit for four minutes, or until heated through and crispy.

Juicy Cheeseburgers

PREP TIME: 5 MINUTES • COOKING TIME: 15 MINUTES • TOTAL COOKING TIME: 20 MINUTES • SERVES: 4

Ingredients

1 pound 93% lean ground beef
1 teaspoon Worcestershire sauce
1 tablespoon burger seasoning
Salt
Pepper
Cooking oil
4 slices cheese
2 buns

Direction:

1 Combine the ground beef, Worcestershire sauce, burger seasoning, and salt & pepper to taste in a large bowl. Spray cooking oil onto the basket of the Salter air fryer. You will just need a short spray. As the patties cook, they will generate oil. Make four patties with the ingredients. Insert the hamburgers into the air fryer. The burgers should fit without stacking, however stacking is acceptable if necessary.

2 Prepare for 8 minutes. Flip the burgers and activate the air fryer. Continue cooking for 3 to 4 minutes. Check the interior of the burgers to determine if they are fully cooked. You can inspect the hue by inserting a knife or fork into the middle. Each burger should have cheese on top. Cook for an additional minute, or until the cheese has melted. Serve on buns with your choice of additional toppings.

Copycat Taco Bell Crunch Wraps

PREP TIME: 10 MINUTES • COOKING TIME: 2 MINUTES • TOTAL COOKING TIME: 15 MINUTES • SERVES: 6

Ingredients

2 C. sour cream
2 C. Mexican blend cheese
2 C. shredded lettuce

12 ounces low-sodium nacho cheese
3 Roma tomatoes
6 12-inch wheat tortillas
1 1/3 C. water
2 packets low-sodium taco seasoning
6 wheat tostadas
2 pounds of lean ground beef

Direction:

1. Ensure your air fryer has been preheated to 400 degrees F.
2. Prepare beef according to the Direction on the taco spice packets.
3. On each tortilla, layer 2/3 cup of prepared beef, 4 tablespoons of cheese, 1 tostada, 1/3 cup of sour cream, 1/3 cup of lettuce, 1/6 cup of tomatoes, and 1/3 cup of cheese.
4. Fold the tortillas' edges and proceed with the remaining ingredients. Lay the folded sides of tortillas down into the air fryer and spray with olive oil.
5. Set the temperature to 400 degrees Fahrenheit and the timer to 2 minutes. Cook for two minutes until brown.

Swedish Meatloaf

PREP TIME: 10 MINUTES • COOKING TIME: 35 MINUTES • TOTAL COOKING TIME: 45 MINUTES • SERVES: 8

Ingredients

¼ pound ground pork or ground beef
1 large egg (omit for egg-free)
½ cup minced onions
¼ cup tomato sauce
2 tablespoons dry mustard
2 cloves garlic, minced
2 teaspoons fine sea salt
1 teaspoon ground black pepper, plus more for garnish
½ cup (1 stick) unsalted butter
½ cup shredded Swiss or mild cheddar cheese (about 2 ounces)
2 ounces cream cheese (¼ cup), softened
⅓ cup beef broth
⅛ teaspoon ground nutmeg
1½ pounds ground beef (85% lean)
Halved cherry tomatoes, for serving (optional)

Direction:

1. Adjust the temperature of the Salter air fryer to 390 degrees Fahrenheit.
2. Combine the ground beef, ground pork, egg, onions, tomato sauce, dry mustard, garlic, and salt & pepper in a large bowl. By hand, properly blend the ingredients.

3 Place the meatloaf mixture in a loaf pan measuring 9 by 5 inches and place it in an air fryer. Cook for 35 minutes, or until the internal temperature reaches 145 degrees Fahrenheit. Check the meatloaf after 25 minutes; if the top is becoming too brown, cover it loosely with aluminum foil to keep it from burning.

4 While the meatloaf is cooking, prepare the sauce by: Constantly whisk the butter in a pot over medium-high heat until it sizzles and brown flecks appear to prevent it from burning. Reduce the heat to low and, while whisking, add the Swiss cheese, cream cheese, broth, and nutmeg. Simmer for a minimum of 10 minutes. The more anything simmers, the more its tastes will develop. Transfer the cooked meatloaf to a serving platter and pour the sauce over it. If preferred, garnish with ground black pepper and serve with cherry tomatoes. Allow the meatloaf to rest for 10 minutes before to slicing to prevent crumbling.

5 Refrigerate leftovers for three days in an airtight container or freeze them for up to one month. Reheat at 350 degrees Fahrenheit for four minutes in an air fryer that has been warmed.

Carne Asada

PREP TIME: 5 MINUTES •COOKING TIME: 8 MINUTES •TOTAL COOKING TIME:2 HOURS 13 MINUTES•SERVES: 4

Ingredients

2 tablespoons coconut vinegar or apple cider vinegar
2 teaspoons orange extract
1 teaspoon stevia glycerite, or ⅛ teaspoon liquid stevia
2 teaspoons ancho chili powder
2 teaspoons fine sea salt
1 teaspoon coriander seeds
1 teaspoon cumin seeds
Sliced radishes
Chopped avocado
Lime slices
1 cup fresh cilantro leaves and stems, plus more for garnish if desired
1 jalapeño pepper, seeded and diced
½ cup lime juice
2 tablespoons avocado oil
1pound skirt steak, cut into 4 equal portions

Direction:

1 To prepare the marinade, combine all of the marinade ingredients until smooth. Place the steak in a shallow dish and pour the marinade over it to ensure total coverage. Cover and refrigerate for two hours or overnight.

2 Spray avocado oil on the Salter air fryer basket. Adjust the temperature of the Salter air fryer to 400 degrees Fahrenheit.

3 Remove the steak from the marinade and arrange it in a single layer into the basket of the

Salter air fryer. Cook for eight minutes, or until the internal temperature reaches 145 degrees Fahrenheit; do not overcook or the meat will turn tough.

4 Remove the steak from the air fryer and let it to rest for 10 minutes on a cutting board before slicing against the grain. If preferred, garnish with cilantro and serve with diced avocado, lime slices, and/or sliced radishes. Refrigerate leftovers for three days in an airtight container or freeze them for up to one month. Reheat at 350 degrees Fahrenheit for four minutes in an air fryer that has been warmed.

Spicy Thai Beef Stir-Fry

PREP TIME: 15 MINUTES • COOKING TIME: 9 MINUTES • TOTAL COOKING TIME: 24 MINUTES • SERVES: 4

Ingredients

2 tablespoons lime juice, divided
⅓ cup crunchy peanut butter
½ cup beef broth
1 tablespoon olive oil
1½ cups broccoli florets
2 cloves garlic, sliced
1pound sirloin steaks, thinly sliced
1 to 2 red chile peppers, sliced

Direction:

1 In a medium bowl, combine the steak and 1 tablespoon of lime juice. Set aside.
2 In a small bowl, thoroughly combine peanut butter and beef broth. Add the beef's liquid to the peanut butter mixture after it has been drained.
3 In a 6-inch metal bowl, combine the steak, broccoli, and olive oil.
4 Shake the basket once while cooking for 3 to 4 minutes, or until the steak is about done and the broccoli is crisp and tender.
5 Stir together the garlic, chili peppers, and peanut butter mixture.
6 Cook the broccoli for 3 to 5 minutes, or until tender and the sauce is boiling.
7 Serve on top of heated rice.

Air Fryer Beef Casserole

PREP TIME: 5 MINUTES • COOKING TIME: 30 MINUTES • TOTAL COOKING TIME: 35 MINUTES • SERVES: 4

Ingredients

6 cups eggs, beaten
1 green bell pepper, seeded and chopped
1 onion, chopped
1-pound ground beef
3 cloves of garlic, minced
3 tablespoons olive oil

Salt and pepper to taste

Direction:

1 The Salter air fryer should be preheated for five minutes. In a baking dish that is compatible with an air fryer, combine ground beef, onion, garlic, olive oil, and bell pepper. season with salt and pepper to taste.
2 Incorporate the beaten eggs and whisk vigorously. Air-fry the dish with the beef and egg combination.
3 Bake for 30 minutes @ 325 ° F.

Salisbury Steak with Mushroom Onion Gravy

PREP TIME: 10 MINUTES • COOKING TIME: 33 MINUTES • TOTAL COOKING TIME: 43 MINUTES • SERVES: 2

Ingredients

¼ teaspoon ground black pepper, plus more for garnish if desired
¾ cup sliced button mushrooms
¼ cup thinly sliced onions
¼ cup unsalted butter, melted (or bacon fat for dairy-free)
½ teaspoon fine sea salt
¼ cup beef broth
½ pound ground beef (85% lean)
¼ cup minced onions, or ½ teaspoon onion powder
2 tablespoons tomato paste
1 tablespoon dry mustard
1 clove garlic, minced, or ¼ teaspoon garlic powder
½ teaspoon fine sea salt
Chopped fresh thyme leaves, for garnish (optional)

Direction:

1 Adjust the temperature of the Salter air fryer to 390 degrees Fahrenheit.
2 Prepare the condiment: Place the mushrooms and onions in an air fryer-compatible casserole dish. Toss the vegetables with the melted butter to coat them. Prepare with salt. Place the dish in the air fryer and cook for 5 minutes, stirring after 2 minutes, or until the onions are tender and the mushrooms are golden brown. Add broth and continue cooking for 10 minutes.
3 While the gravy cooks, prepare the steaks as follows: Mix the ground beef, onions, tomato paste, dry mustard, garlic, salt, and pepper thoroughly in a large bowl. Form the mixture into two oval burgers.
4 The hamburger patties should be placed on the mushroom gravy. Cook for 10 minutes, then flip the patties and cook for an additional 2 to 5 minutes, or until the beef reaches an internal temperature of 145 degrees Fahrenheit.
5 Transfer the steaks to a serving plate and drizzle them with the gravy. If preferred, garnish

with ground black pepper and chopped fresh thyme. Refrigerate leftovers for three days in an airtight container or freeze them for up to one month. Reheat at 350 degrees Fahrenheit for four minutes in an air fryer that has been warmed.

Fajita Meatball Lettuce Wraps

PREP TIME: 10 MINUTES • COOKING TIME: 10 MINUTES • TOTAL COOKING TIME: 20 MINUTES • SERVES: 4

Ingredients

Pico de gallo or salsa
1 pound ground beef (85% lean)
½ cup salsa, plus more for serving if desired
¼ cup chopped onions
¼ cup diced green or red bell peppers
1 large egg, beaten
1 teaspoon fine sea salt
½ teaspoon chili powder
½ teaspoon ground cumin
1 clove garlic, minced
FOR SERVING (OPTIONAL):
8 leaves Boston lettuce
Lime slices

Direction:

1 Spray avocado oil on the Salter air fryer basket. Heat the Salter air fryer to 350 degrees Fahrenheit before use. In a large mixing bowl, thoroughly combine all the ingredients.
2 Form eight meatballs measuring 1 inch from the mixture.
3 Place the meatballs in the basket of the air fryer, leaving some space between each one. Cook for 10 minutes, or until the interior is no longer pink and the temperature hits 145 degrees Fahrenheit. Serve each meatball on a lettuce leaf with salsa or pico de gallo, if desired. Served with lime slices upon request. Refrigerate leftovers in an airtight container for up to three days, or freeze for up to one month. Reheat at 350 degrees Fahrenheit for four minutes in an air fryer that has been warmed.

Chimichurri Skirt Steak

PREP TIME: 10 MINUTES • COOKING TIME: 8 MINUTES • TOTAL COOKING TIME: 18 MINUTES • SERVES: 2

Ingredients

¾ cup Oil
2 x 8 oz Skirt Steak
1 cup Finely Chopped Parsley

¼ cup Finely Chopped Mint
2 Tbsp Fresh Oregano (Washed & finely chopped)
3 Finely Chopped Cloves of Garlic
1 Tsp Red Pepper Flakes (Crushed)
1 Tbsp Ground Cumin
1 Tsp Cayenne Pepper
2 Tsp Smoked Paprika
1 Tsp Salt
¼ Tsp Pepper
3 Tbsp Red Wine Vinegar

Direction:

1. Except for the steak, thoroughly combine the remaining ingredients in a bowl.
2. Place a quarter cup of the mixture along with the steak in a plastic bag and refrigerate overnight (2–24 hours).
3. Allow the bag to remain at room temperature for a minimum of 30 minutes before inserting it in the Air fryer. Before cooking to medium-rare (8–10 minutes), preheat the pan to 390 degrees Fahrenheit for a minute or two.
4. Before serving, place 2 tablespoons of the chimichurri mixture on top of each steak.

Reuben Fritters

PREP TIME: 10 MINUTES • COOKING TIME: 16 MINUTES • TOTAL COOKING TIME: 17 MINUTES • SERVES: 1 dozen fritters

Ingredients

1 (8-ounce) package cream cheese, softened
½ cup finely shredded Swiss cheese (about 2 ounces)
¼ cup sauerkraut
1 cup pork dust or powdered Parmesan cheese
Chopped fresh thyme, for garnish
Thousand Island Dipping Sauce for serving
2 cups finely diced cooked corned beef
Cornichons, for serving (optional)

Direction:

1. Spray avocado oil on the Salter air fryer basket. Adjust the temperature of the Salter air fryer to 390 degrees Fahrenheit. Combine the corned beef, cream cheese, Swiss cheese, and sauerkraut in a large bowl. Form twelve 112-inch balls from the corned beef mixture
2. The pork dust should be placed in a small basin. Roll the corned beef balls in the pork dust, then form a thick crust around each ball with your hands.
3. Place six balls evenly spaced in the air fryer basket and cook for eight minutes, or until golden and crispy. Allow them to cool slightly before taking them from the air fryer (the fritters are

extremely soft when the cheese has melted; they are easier to handle once the cheese has solidified). Repeat for the remainder of the fritters.

4 If preferred, garnish with chopped fresh thyme and serve with dipping sauce and cornichons. Refrigerate leftovers in an airtight container for up to three days, or freeze for up to one month. Reheat at 350 degrees Fahrenheit for four minutes in an air fryer that has been warmed.

Charred Onions And Steak Cube BBQ

PREP TIME: 5 MINUTES • COOKING TIME: 40 MINUTES • TOTAL COOKING TIME: 45 MINUTES • SERVES: 3

Ingredients

1 cup red onions, cut into wedges
1 tablespoon dry mustard
1 tablespoon olive oil
1-pound boneless beef sirloin, cut into cubes
Salt and pepper to taste

Direction:

1 The air fryer should be preheated to 390 degrees Fahrenheit.
2 Insert the auxiliary grill pan into the air fryer.
3 Toss the items with the seasonings in a bowl until everything is uniformly coated.
4 Cook on the grill pan for forty minutes.
5 Stir halfway during the cooking period to ensure even cooking.

Steak and Mushroom Gravy

PREP TIME: 15 MINUTES • COOKING TIME: 15 MINUTES • TOTAL COOKING TIME: 30 MINUTES • SERVES: 4

Ingredients

1/3 cup flour
4 cubed steaks
2 large eggs
1/2 dozen mushrooms
4 tablespoons unsalted butter
4 tablespoons black pepper
2 tablespoons salt
1/2 teaspoon onion powder
1/2 teaspoon garlic powder
1/4 teaspoon cayenne powder
1 1/4 teaspoons paprika
1 1/2 cups whole milk

2 tablespoons vegetable oil

Direction:

1. Combine 1/2 cup of flour and a pinch of ground black pepper in a shallow basin or plate. Beat two eggs with a teaspoon of salt and pepper in a bowl.
2. In a second shallow bowl, combine the remaining flour with pepper to taste, garlic powder, paprika, cayenne pepper, and onion powder.
3. Cut mushrooms into small pieces and set aside. Press the steak into the first basin of flour, then into the egg, and finally into the second dish of flour until well coated.
4. Air fry steak at 360 degrees for 15 minutes, turning halfway through cooking. While the steak is cooking, melt the butter over medium heat and sauté the mushrooms. Add four tablespoons of the flour and pepper combination to the saucepan and whisk until there are no more flour lumps. Add full milk, then simmer. Serve over steak for breakfast, lunch, or dinner.

Country Fried Steak

PREP TIME: 5 MINUTES • COOKING TIME: 12 MINUTES • TOTAL COOKING TIME: 20 MINUTES • SERVES: 2

Ingredients

1 C. almond flour
3 beaten eggs
1 tsp. pepper
2 C. almond milk
2 tbsp. almond flour
6 ounces ground sausage meat
1 tsp. pepper
1 tsp. salt
1 tsp. garlic powder
1 tsp. onion powder
1 C. panko breadcrumbs
6 ounces sirloin steak, pounded till thin

Direction:

1. Season panko breadcrumbs with spices. Coat steak with flour, then egg, and finally seasoned panko mixture. Insert into the air fryer basket.
2. Set temperature to 370 degrees Fahrenheit and timer to 12 minutes. To make sausage gravy, cook and drain sausage, reserving 2 tablespoons of grease. Add flour to the sausage and combine thoroughly. Gradually stir in milk while heating over medium to high heat until it thickens. Cook the mixture for three minutes longer with pepper. Serve steak with a gravy topping and enjoy.

Greek Stuffed Tenderloin

PREP TIME: 10 MINUTES • COOKING TIME: 10 MINUTES • TOTAL COOKING TIME: 20 MINUTES • SERVES: 4

Ingredients

Extra-virgin olive oil
Sprigs of fresh rosemary
1½ pounds venison or beef tenderloin, pounded to ¼ inch thick
3 teaspoons fine sea salt
1 teaspoon ground black pepper
2 ounces creamy goat cheese
½ cup crumbled feta cheese (about 2 ounces)
¼ cup finely chopped onions
2 cloves garlic, minced
FOR GARNISH/SERVING (OPTIONAL):
Prepared yellow mustard
Halved cherry tomatoes
Lavender flowers

Direction:

1. Spray avocado oil on the Salter air fryer basket. Adjust the temperature of the Salter air fryer to 400 degrees Fahrenheit. Season the tenderloin on all sides with salt and pepper.
2. In a medium-sized mixing bowl, combine goat cheese, feta, onion, and garlic. The mixture should be placed in the center of the tenderloin. Beginning at the end closest to you, roll the tenderloin tightly into a jelly roll shape. Tightly bind the coiled tenderloin with kitchen twine.
3. Place the meat in the basket of the Salter air fryer and cook for five minutes. Cook the meat for a further 5 minutes, or until the internal temperature reaches 135 degrees Fahrenheit for medium-rare. Spread a line of prepared yellow mustard on a serving dish, then place the meat next to it and, if desired, garnish with halved cherry tomatoes. If desired, drizzle olive oil and garnish with rosemary sprigs and lavender flowers.
4. Freshest served. Refrigerate leftovers in an airtight jar for three days. Reheat at 350 degrees Fahrenheit for four minutes in an air fryer that has been warmed.

Warming Winter Beef with Celery

PREP TIME: 5 MINUTES • COOKING TIME: 12 MINUTES • TOTAL COOKING TIME: 15 MINUTES • SERVES: 4

Ingredients

9 ounces tender beef, chopped
1/2 cup leeks, chopped

1/2 cup celery stalks, chopped
2 cloves garlic, smashed
2 tablespoons red cooking wine
3/4 cup cream of celery soup
2 sprigs rosemary, chopped
1/4 teaspoon smoked paprika
3/4 teaspoons salt
1/4 teaspoon black pepper, or to taste

Direction:

1. Cook the beef, leeks, celery, and garlic at 390 degrees Fahrenheit for roughly 5 minutes.
2. Once the beef begins to get soft, add the wine and soup. Add rosemary, smoked paprika, salt, and black pepper to taste. Continue cooking for 7 minutes.

Black and Blue Burgers

PREP TIME: 5 MINUTES • COOKING TIME:10
• TOTAL COOKING TIME: 15 MINUTES • SERVES: 2
Ingredients

6 red onion slices
½ teaspoon fine sea salt
¼ teaspoon ground black pepper
¼ teaspoon garlic powder
¼ teaspoon onion powder
¼ teaspoon smoked paprika
2 (¼-pound) hamburger patties, ½ inch thick
½ cup crumbled blue cheese (about 2 ounces)
2 Hamburger Buns
2 tablespoons mayonnaise
2 Boston lettuce leaves

Direction:

1. Spray avocado oil on the Salter air fryer basket. Heat the Salter air fryer to 360 degrees Fahrenheit before use. In a small bowl, combine the salt, pepper, and spices. Utilizing the seasoning combination, season the burgers on both sides.
2. Place the patties in the basket of the Salter air fryer and cook for 7 minutes, or until the internal temperature reaches 145 degrees Fahrenheit. Melt the blue cheese on top of the patties by cooking for an additional minute. Allow the burgers to rest for 5 minutes after removing them from the air fryer. Cut the buns in half and spread mayonnaise on two sides of each half. Increase the temperature to 400 degrees Fahrenheit and lay the buns, cut side up, in the basket of the Salter air fryer. Toast the rolls for one to two minutes, until they are golden brown. Place the buns on a serving plate after removing them from the air fryer. Place the patties on the buns and top each with three slices of red onion and a leaf of lettuce.

Cheesy Ground Beef And Mac Taco Casserole

PREP TIME: 10 MINUTES • COOKING TIME: 25 MINUTES • TOTAL COOKING TIME: 35 MINUTES • SERVES: 5

Ingredients

1-ounce shredded Cheddar cheese
1-ounce shredded Monterey Jack cheese
2 tablespoons chopped green onions
1/2 (10.75 ounce) can condensed tomato soup
1/2-pound lean ground beef
1/2 cup crushed tortilla chips
1/4-pound macaroni, cooked according to manufacturer's Direction
1/4 cup chopped onion
1/4 cup sour cream (optional)
1/2 (1.25 ounce) package taco seasoning mix
1/2 (14.5 ounce) can diced tomatoes

Direction:

1. Spray the baking pan of the air fryer lightly with cooking spray. Add onion and ground beef. For 10 minutes, cook at 360 degrees Fahrenheit. Stir and break apart ground meat halfway through cooking. Add taco spice, tomato soup, and diced tomatoes. Blend well. Mix in pasta. The addition of tortilla chip crumbs. Sprinkle cheese.
2. Cook for 15 minutes at 390 °F, or until the cheese is melted and the tops are gently browned. Serve with pleasure.

Meat Lovers' Pizza

PREP TIME: 10 MINUTES • COOKING TIME: 12 MINUTES • TOTAL COOKING TIME: 22 MINUTES • SERVES: 2

Ingredients

1 pre-prepared 7-inch pizza pie crust, defrosted if necessary.
1/3 cup of marinara sauce.
2 ounces of grilled steak, sliced into bite-sized pieces
2 ounces of salami, sliced fine
2 ounces of pepperoni, sliced fine
¼ cup of American cheese
¼ cup of shredded mozzarella cheese

Direction:

1. The air fryer should be preheated to 350 degrees Fahrenheit. Place the pizza dough flat on a sheet of parchment paper or aluminum foil that is large enough to fit the entire pie crust but small enough to leave the corners of the air frying basket uncovered for air circulation.

Using a fork, pierce the pizza dough's surface multiple times; this will allow air to circulate throughout the crust and ensure uniform cooking. With a large soup spoon, ladle the marinara sauce onto the pizza dough and spread it evenly in expanding circles around the crust's surface. Leave at least a half-inch of unbaked dough around the edges for an extra-crispy initial bite. Distribute the steak, salami, and pepperoni slices evenly over the sauce-coated dough, then sprinkle the cheese on top in an even layer.

2 Set the timer on the Salter air fryer to 12 minutes, and set the pizza wrapped in foil or paper on the basket's surface. Again, leave the sides of the basket open to allow for proper air circulation, and avoid touching the surface with your bare fingers. When the Air fryer shuts off after 12 minutes, the cheese should be properly melted and faintly browned, and the pie crust should be golden brown. Using one or two spatulas, remove the pizza from the basket of the Salter air fryer and put on a serving tray. Wait a few minutes until the pie has cooled sufficiently before slicing and serving.

Mushroom and Swiss Burgers

PREP TIME: 5 MINUTES • COOKING TIME: 15 MINUTES • TOTAL COOKING TIME: 20 MINUTES• SERVES: 2

Ingredients

1 teaspoon fine sea salt, divided
¼ teaspoon garlic powder
¼ teaspoon ground black pepper
2 slices Swiss cheese (omit for dairy-free)
¼ teaspoon onion powder
¼ teaspoon smoked paprika
2 (¼-pound) hamburger patties, ½ inch thick
2 large portobello mushrooms
Condiments of choice, such as Ranch Dressing, prepared yellow mustard, or mayonnaise, for serving

Direction:

1 Heat the Salter air fryer to 360 degrees Fahrenheit before use. Remove and clean the stems from the portobello mushrooms. The mushrooms should be sprayed on all sides with avocado oil and seasoned with a half teaspoon of salt.

2 Place the mushrooms in the basket of the Salter air fryer and cook for seven to eight minutes, or until soft to the touch and easily pierced with a fork.

3 In a separate bowl, combine the remaining 12 teaspoon of salt, garlic powder, pepper, onion powder, and paprika while the mushrooms cook. The hamburger patties are dusted with the spice mixture. When the mushrooms are cooked, remove them from the air fryer and arrange them cap-side down on a serving tray.

4 Place the hamburger patties in the air fryer and cook for seven minutes, or until an internal temperature of 145 degrees Fahrenheit is reached for a medium-done burger. Each burger should be topped with a slice of Swiss cheese and cooked for an additional minute to melt the cheese. Place the burgers on top of the mushrooms and top with the condiments of your choice. Freshest ingredients served.

Air Fryer Steak Tips

PREP TIME: 5 MINUTES • COOKING TIME: 8 MINUTES • TOTAL COOKING TIME: 1 HOUR 13 MINUTES• SERVES: 4

Ingredients

⅓ cup soy sauce
1 cup water
¼ cup freshly squeezed lemon juice
3 tablespoons brown sugar
1 teaspoon garlic powder
1 teaspoon ground ginger
1 teaspoon dried parsley
2 pounds steak tips, cut into 1-inch cubes

Direction:

1 In a large bowl, mix the marinade ingredients. In a mixing bowl, combine soy sauce, water, lemon juice, brown sugar, garlic powder, ginger, and parsley. Cover and refrigerate the meat in the marinade for at least one hour. Adjust the temperature of the Salter air fryer to 400 degrees Fahrenheit. Spray olive oil onto the basket of the Salter air fryer.

2 When the steak has finished marinating, insert it in the oiled basket of an air fryer.

3 Set the timer for 4 minutes and cook the food. Use tongs to turn the meat. Reset the timer and continue cooking for another 4 minutes.

Creamy Burger & Potato Bake

PREP TIME: 5 MINUTES • COOKING TIME: 55 MINUTES • TOTAL COOKING TIME: 60 MINUTES • SERVES: 3

Ingredients

freshly ground pepper, to taste
1/2 (10.75 ounce) can condensed cream of mushroom soup
1/2-pound lean ground beef
1-1/2 cups peeled and thinly sliced potatoes
1/2 cup shredded Cheddar cheese
1/4 cup chopped onion
salt to taste
1/4 cup and 2 tablespoons milk

Direction:

1 Spray the baking pan of the air fryer lightly with cooking spray. Integrate ground beef. For 10 minutes, cook at 360 degrees Fahrenheit. Stir and crush ingredients halfway through cooking. In the meantime, whisk together pepper, salt, milk, onion, and mushroom soup in a basin. Blend well. Drain the grease from the ground beef and place the meat on a platter. In the same air fryer baking pan, put one-half of the potatoes, one-half of the soup mixture, and

one-half of the meat. Repeat actions. Cover the dish with foil.

2 Prepare for 30 minutes. Remove foil and boil potatoes for a further 15 minutes, or until tender. Serve with pleasure.

Beef Stroganoff

PREP TIME: 10 MINUTES • COOKING TIME: 14 MINUTES • TOTAL COOKING TIME: 24 MINUTES • SERVES: 4

Ingredients

Salt and Pepper to taste
9 Ozs Tender Beef
1 Onion, chopped
1 Tbsp Paprika
3/4 Cup Sour Cream
Baking Dish

Direction:

1 The air fryer should be heated to 390 degrees Celsius.

2 The beef is chopped and marinated with paprika. Add the chopped onions to the baking dish and heat for roughly two minutes in the Air fryer. Once the onions are translucent, add the steak and simmer for five minutes. Once the beef begins to get soft, add the sour cream and simmer for an additional seven minutes. At this time, the liquid should have decreased in volume. Add salt and pepper before serving.

SEAFOOD RECIPES

Coconut Shrimp

PREP TIME: 5 MINUTES • COOKING TIME: 10 MINUTES • TOTAL COOKING TIME: 15 MINUTES • SERVES: 3

Ingredients

1 tbsp. coconut flour
1 C. unsweetened, dried coconut
1 egg white
1 C. almond flour
1 C. panko breadcrumbs
12 raw large shrimp

Direction:

1. Place the shrimp on paper towels for draining.
2. Combine coconut and panko breadcrumbs. Then, combine coconut and almond flours in a separate basin. Set to the side. Dip shrimp into flour mixture, then into egg white, and then into coconut mixture. Place into air fryer basket. Continue with the remaining shrimp.
3. Set temperature to 350°F, and set time to 10 minutes. Turn halfway through cooking process.

Air Fryer Cajun Shrimp

PREP TIME: 5 MINUTES • COOKING TIME: 6 MINUTES • TOTAL COOKING TIME: 11 MINUTES • SERVES: 2

Ingredients

1 teaspoon Old Bay seasoning
½ teaspoon smoked paprika
2 tablespoons olive oil
12 ounces uncooked medium shrimp, peeled and deveined
1 teaspoon cayenne pepper
1 teaspoon salt

Direction:

1. Preheat the Salter air fryer to 390 degrees Fahrenheit.
2. In the meantime, combine the shrimp, cayenne pepper, Old Bay, paprika, olive oil, and salt in a medium mixing bowl. Toss the shrimp in the oil and spices until the shrimp is thoroughly coated with both.
3. Place the shrimp in the air fryer basket. Set the timer and steam for 3 minutes. Remove the

drawer and shake, so the shrimp redistribute in the basket for equal frying. Reset the timer and steam for another 3 minutes. Determine if the shrimp are cooked. When they are fully cooked, their flesh will become opaque. Add additional time if needed. Plate, serve, and enjoy!

Grilled Salmon

PREP TIME: 5 MINUTES • COOKING TIME: 10 MINUTES • TOTAL COOKING TIME: 15 MINUTES • SERVES: 3

Ingredients

1/3 Cup Soy Sauce
1/3 Cup Sugar
2 Salmon Fillets
1/2 Tsp Lemon Pepper
1/2 Tsp Garlic Powder
Salt and Pepper
1 Tbsp Olive Oil

Direction:

1 The salmon fillets are seasoned with lemon pepper, garlic powder, and salt. In a shallow bowl, combine olive oil, soy sauce, and sugar with a third cup of water. Place salmon the bowl and soak in the sauce. Cover with cling film and allow to marinate in the refrigerator for at least an hour

1 Heat the Salter air fryer to 350 degrees Fahrenheit.

2 Place salmon in the Air fryer and cook for at least 10 minutes, or until tender. Serve with lemon wedges

Homemade Air Fried Crab Cake Sliders

PREP TIME: 5 MINUTES • COOKING TIME: 10 MINUTES • TOTAL COOKING TIME: 15 MINUTES • SERVES: 4

Ingredients

½ teaspoon freshly ground black pepper
1 large egg
2 tablespoons mayonnaise
1 teaspoon dry mustard
4 slider buns
1pound crabmeat, shredded
¼ cup bread crumbs
2 teaspoons dried parsley
1 teaspoon salt
Sliced tomato, lettuce leaves, and rémoulade sauce, for topping

Direction:

1. *Spray the basket of the Salter air fryer with olive oil, or spray a baking sheet sized for the air fryer with olive oil or cooking spray. In a medium mixing bowl, combine the crabmeat, bread crumbs, parsley, salt, pepper, egg, mayonnaise, and dry mustard. Mix well. Form four equal crab patties from the crab mixture. (If the patties are too wet, add an additional 1 to 2 tablespoons of bread crumbs.) Place the crab cakes directly into the greased air fryer basket, or on the greased baking sheet set into the air fryer basket.*
2. *Set the Salter AF's temperature to 400 degrees Fahrenheit. Set the timer and fry for 5 minutes. Flip the crab cakes. Reset the timer and fry the crab cakes for 5 minutes more. Serve on slider buns with sliced tomato, lettuce, and rémoulade sauce.*

Air Fried Lobster Tails

PREP TIME: 5 MINUTES • COOKING TIME: 8 MINUTES • TOTAL COOKING TIME: 13 MINUTES • SERVES: 2

Ingredients

1 teaspoon salt
1 tablespoon minced fresh chives
2 tablespoons unsalted butter, melted
1 tablespoon minced garlic
2 (4- to 6-ounce) frozen lobster tails

Direction:

1 Combine the butter, garlic, salt, and chives in a small bowl.

2 Butterfly the lobster tail: Starting at the meaty end of the tail, use kitchen shears to cut down the middle of the top shell. Stop when you reach the fanned, wide section of the tail. Carefully spread apart the meat and the shell along the cut line, but keep the meat attached where it connects to the wide part of the tail. Use your hand to gently separate the meat from the shell's base. Lift the meat up and out of the shell (keeping it attached at the wide end). Close the shell beneath the meat so that the meat rests atop the shell.

3 Place the lobster in the Salter air fryer basket and generously brush the butter mixture over the meat.

4 Set the temperature of your Salter AF to 380°F. Set the timer for four minutes and steam.

5 Open the air fryer and rotate the lobster tails. Coat them with additional butter mixture. Reset the timer and steam for 4 minutes more. The lobster is done when the meat is opaque.

Crispy Paprika Fish Fillets

PREP TIME: 5 MINUTES • COOKING TIME: 15 MINUTES • TOTAL COOKING TIME: 20 MINUTES • SERVES: 4

Ingredients

1 teaspoon paprika
1/2 teaspoon ground black pepper
1 teaspoon celery seed
2 fish fillets, halved
1/2 cup seasoned breadcrumbs
1 tablespoon balsamic vinegar
1/2 teaspoon seasoned salt
1 egg, beaten

Direction:

1. Incorporate the breadcrumbs, vinegar, salt, paprika, black pepper, and celery seeds into a food processor. Process for about 30 seconds.
2. Coat the fish fillets with the beaten egg; then, coat them with the breadcrumbs mixture.
3. Cook at 350 degrees F for about 15 minutes.

Bacon Wrapped Shrimp

PREP TIME: 5 MINUTES • COOKING TIME: 5 MINUTES • TOTAL COOKING TIME: 10 MINUTES • SERVES: 4

Ingredients

1¼ pound tiger shrimp, peeled and deveined
1 pound bacon

Direction:

1. Wrap each shrimp in a bacon slice.
2. Refrigerate for roughly twenty minutes. Preheat the Salter air fryer to 390 degrees F.
3. Arrange the shrimp in the Air fryer basket. Cook for roughly 5 to 7 minutes.

Bacon-Wrapped Scallops

PREP TIME: 5 MINUTES • COOKING TIME: 10 MINUTES • TOTAL COOKING TIME: 15 MINUTES • SERVES: 4

Ingredients

8 toothpicks
Salt
16 sea scallops
8 slices bacon, cut in half
Freshly ground black pepper

Direction:

1. Using paper towels, blot the scallops dry.

2 Wrap each scallop with a half slice of bacon. Secure the bacon with a toothpick.
3 Place the scallops in a single layer in the air fryer. (You may have to cook the scallops in multiple batches.)
4 Spray the scallops with olive oil, and season them with salt and pepper.
5 Set the temperature of your Salter AF to 370°F. Set the timer for 5 minutes and fry the food.
6 To turn the scallops.
7 Reset the timer and cook the scallops for 5 minutes more.
8 Using tongs, remove the scallops from the air fryer basket. Plating, serving, and enjoying!

Air Fryer Salmon

PREP TIME: 5 MINUTES • COOKING TIME: 10 MINUTES • TOTAL COOKING TIME: 15 MINUTES • SERVES: 2

Ingredients

½ tsp. smoked paprika
½ tsp. salt
½ tsp. garlic powder
Salmon

Direction:

1. Combine spices and sprinkle them on salmon. Place salmon with seasonings in the Air fryer.
2. Close crisping lid. Set temperature to 400°F, and set time to 10 minutes.

Lemon Pepper, Butter, And Cajun Cod

PREP TIME: 5 MINUTES • COOKING TIME: 12 MINUTES4 • TOTAL COOKING TIME: 17 MINUTES • SERVES: 2

Ingredients

1 teaspoon salt
½ teaspoon freshly ground black pepper
2 tablespoons unsalted butter, melted
2 (8-ounce) cod fillets, cut to fit into the air fryer basket
1 tablespoon Cajun seasoning
½ teaspoon lemon pepper
1 lemon, cut into 4 wedges

Direction:

1 Spray olive oil onto the basket of the Salter air fryer. Place the fillets on a serving dish. Combine the Cajun seasoning, lemon pepper, salt, and pepper in a small bowl.

2 Rub the spice mixture onto the fish.
3 Place the fish in the air fryer basket that has been oiled. Coat each fillet's surface with melted butter.
4 Set the Salter AF's temperature to 360 degrees Fahrenheit. Set the timer for 6 minutes and bake. After six minutes, open the drawer of your air fryer and flip the fish. Brush each fillet with additional melted butter.
5 Reset the timer and bake for a further 6 minutes. Apply freshly squeezed lemon juice to the fillets.

Steamed Salmon & Sauce

PREP TIME: 5 MINUTES • COOKING TIME: 10 MINUTES • TOTAL COOKING TIME: 15 MINUTES • SERVES: 2

Ingredients

½ cup Plain Greek Yogurt
½ cup Sour Cream
2 Tbsp Finely Chopped Dill (Keep a bit for garnishing)
1 cup Water
2 x 6 oz Fresh Salmon
2 Tsp Vegetable Oil
A Pinch of Salt for Each Fish
A Pinch of Salt to Taste

Direction:

1 Pour the water into the bottom of the fryer and start heating to 285° F.
2 Drizzle oil over the fish and spread it. Salt the fish to taste.
3 Now pop it into the fryer for 10 min.
4 In the meantime, mix the yogurt, cream, dill and a little of salt to produce the sauce. When the fish is done, serve with the sauce and garnish with sprigs of dill.

Salmon Patties

PREP TIME: 5 MINUTES • COOKING TIME: 10 MINUTES • TOTAL COOKING TIME: 15 MINUTES • SERVES: 4

Ingredients

1 teaspoon dried dill
½ teaspoon freshly ground black pepper
1 teaspoon salt
1 (14.75-ounce) can wild salmon, drained
1 large egg
¼ cup diced onion
½ cup bread crumbs
1 teaspoon Old Bay seasoning

Direction:

1 Spray the Salter air fryer basket with olive oil. Put the salmon in a medium bowl and remove any bones or skin. Add the egg, onion, bread crumbs, dill, pepper, salt, and Old Bay seasoning and combine thoroughly. Form the salmon mixture into 4 equal patties. Place the patties in the greased air fryer basket.

2 Set the temperature of your Salter AF to 370°F. Set the timer and grill for 5 minutes. Flip the patties. Reset the timer and grill the patties for 5 minutes more. Plate, serve, and enjoy.

Sweet And Savory Breaded Shrimp

PREP TIME: 5 MINUTES • COOKING TIME: 20 MINUTES • TOTAL COOKING TIME: 25 MINUTES • SERVES: 2

Ingredients

1 teaspoon of ginger-garlic paste
½ teaspoon of turmeric powder
½ teaspoon of red chili powder
½ teaspoon of cumin powder
½ teaspoon of black pepper powder
½ pound of fresh shrimp, peeled from their shells and rinsed
2 raw eggs
½ cup of breadcrumbs (we like Panko, but any brand or home recipe will do)
½ white onion, peeled and rinsed and finely chopped
½ teaspoon of dry mango powder
Pinch of salt

Direction:

1 Cover the basket of the Air fryer with tin foil, leaving the edges open to enable air circulation.

2 Preheat the air fryer to 350 degrees Fahrenheit. In a large mixing bowl, whisk the eggs until they are frothy and the yolks and whites are thoroughly blended. Submerge the shrimp completely in the egg mixture. In a separate mixing bowl, thoroughly combine the bread crumbs with the dry ingredients. Coat the egg-coated shrimp with the dry mixture so that they are completely covered, then lay them on the foil-lined air fryer basket.

3 Set the timer on the air fryer to 20 minutes. Halfway through the cooking time, jiggle the air fryer's handle to agitate the breaded shrimp and ensure uniform frying. When the fryer shuts off after twenty minutes, the shrimp will be fully cooked and their breading will be golden brown and delicious! Using tongs, remove the food from the air fryer and place it on a dish to cool.

Healthy Fish and Chips

PREP TIME: 5 MINUTES • COOKING TIME: 15 MINUTES • TOTAL COOKING TIME: 20 MINUTES • SERVES: 3

Ingredients

2 tbsp. almond flour
4-6 ounce tilapia fillets
Old Bay seasoning
½ C. panko breadcrumbs
1 egg
Frozen crinkle cut fries

Direction:

1 Add almond flour to one bowl, egg to another bowl, and panko breadcrumbs seasoned with Old Bay to a third bowl. Coat fish in flour, followed by egg, and then breadcrumbs. Place covered fish and fries in an air fryer.
2 Set temperature to 390 degrees Fahrenheit and timer to 15 minutes.

Indian Fish Fingers

PREP TIME: 35 MINUTES • COOKING TIME: 15 MINUTES • TOTAL COOKING TIME: 50 MINUTES • SERVES: 4

Ingredients

1/2 teaspoon paprika
Generous pinch of black pepper
Salt to taste
3/4 tablespoons lemon juice
3/4 teaspoons garam masala powder
1/3 teaspoon rosemary
1/2pound fish fillet
1 tablespoon finely chopped fresh mint leaves or any fresh herbs
1/3 cup bread crumbs
1 teaspoon ginger garlic paste or ginger and garlic powders
1 hot green chili finely chopped
1 egg

Direction:

1 Start by removing the fish's skin, cleaning it, and patting it dry. The fish was cut into fingers. Mix all ingredients except the fish, mint, and bread crumbs in a medium bowl. Refrigerate the fingers for 30 minutes after burying them in the mixture. Remove the bowl from the refrigerator and combine with mint leaves. In a second bowl, whisk the egg, and in a fourth bowl, place the bread crumbs. Dip the fingers in the egg, then throw them in the bowl of bread crumbs.
2 15 minutes at 360 degrees, turning fingers halfway through.

Lemon, Garlic, And Herb Salmon

PREP TIME: 5 MINUTES • COOKING TIME: 10 MINUTES

• TOTAL COOKING TIME: 15 MINUTES • SERVES: 4
Ingredients

1 tablespoon minced fresh parsley
1 teaspoon minced fresh dill
1 teaspoon salt
½ teaspoon freshly ground black pepper
3 tablespoons unsalted butter
1 garlic clove, minced, or ½ teaspoon garlic powder
1 teaspoon salt
2 tablespoons freshly squeezed lemon juice
4 (4-ounce) salmon fillets

Direction:

1 Line the basket of the Salter air fryer with parchment paper.
2 In a small mixing bowl that can be heated in the microwave, combine the butter, garlic, salt, lemon juice, parsley, dill, and pepper. Place the bowl in the microwave and heat on low for approximately 45 seconds, or until the butter is completely melted. Meanwhile, place the salmon fillets in the air fryer basket coated with parchment paper. Pour the sauce on top of the fish.
3 Set the Salter AF's temperature to 400 degrees Fahrenheit. Set the timer for 10 minutes and bake. In order to avoid overcooking the salmon, begin checking for doneness after approximately 8 minutes. When the flesh is opaque and flakes readily with a fork, salmon is cooked.

Shrimp Scampi

PREP TIME: 5 MINUTES • COOKING TIME: 8 MINUTES
• TOTAL COOKING TIME: 13 MINUTES • SERVES: 4
Ingredients

1 teaspoon red pepper flakes
1pound large shrimp, peeled and deveined, tails removed
¼ cup unsalted butter (or butter-flavored coconut oil for dairy-free)
2 tablespoons fish stock or chicken broth
1 tablespoon lemon juice
2 cloves garlic, minced
2 tablespoons chopped fresh basil leaves
1 tablespoon chopped fresh parsley, plus more for garnish
Fresh basil sprigs, for garnish

Direction:

1 Preheat the air fryer to 350 degrees Fahrenheit. In a 6-by-3-inch pan, combine the butter, fish stock, lemon juice, garlic, basil, parsley, and red pepper flakes, then set in the air fryer.

2 Cook for three minutes, or until the garlic becomes fragrant and tender.
3 Stir the shrimp into the sauce to coat the shrimp. Cook the shrimp for 5 minutes, or until pink, stirring after 3 minutes. Before serving, garnish with fresh basil stems and chopped parsley. Refrigerate leftovers in an airtight jar for up to four days. Reheat in a preheated air fryer at 400 degrees Fahrenheit for approximately three minutes.

Simple Scallops

PREP TIME: 5 MINUTES • COOKING TIME: 4 MINUTES • TOTAL COOKING TIME: 9 MINUTES • SERVES: 2

Ingredients

¾ teaspoon ground black pepper, plus more for garnish if desired
12 medium sea scallops
1 teaspoon fine sea salt
Fresh thyme leaves, for garnish (optional)

Direction:

1 Spray avocado oil on the basket of the Salter air fryer. Preheat the Salter air fryer to 390 degrees Fahrenheit. Rinse the scallops and pat them dry well. Salt and pepper the scallops after spraying them with avocado oil.
2 Place them in the air fryer basket, spacing them apart (if necessary, work in batches if using a smaller air fryer). Cook for two minutes before flipping and cooking for a further two minutes, or until opaque and fully done. If preferred, garnish with ground black pepper and thyme leaves. Freshest served. Refrigerate leftovers in an airtight jar for up to three days. Reheat in a preheated air fryer at 350°F for two minutes, or until thoroughly heated.

Quick Paella

PREP TIME: 7 MINUTES • COOKING TIME: 15 MINUTES • TOTAL COOKING TIME: 22 MINUTES • SERVES: 4

Ingredients

½ teaspoon dried thyme
1 cup frozen cooked small shrimp
½ cup frozen baby peas
1 (10-ounce) package frozen cooked rice, thawed
1 (6-ounce) jar artichoke hearts, drained and chopped
¼ cup vegetable broth
½ teaspoon turmeric
1 tomato, diced

Direction:

1 Rice, artichoke hearts, vegetable broth, turmeric, and thyme are combined in a 6-by-6-by-2-inch skillet with gentle stirring.
2 Place the rice in the Air fryer and bake for 8 to 9 minutes, or until heated. Remove from the air

fryer and toss in the shrimp, peas, and tomato with care. Cook until the shrimp and peas are heated and the paella is boiling, about 5 to 8 minutes.

Tuna Melt Croquettes

PREP TIME: 5 MINUTES • COOKING TIME: 10 MINUTES • TOTAL COOKING TIME: 15 MINUTES • SERVES: 1

Ingredients

2 teaspoons prepared yellow mustard
1 large egg
1½ cups pork dust or powdered Parmesan cheese
Fresh dill, for garnish (optional)
Cherry tomatoes
Mayonnaise
2 (5-ounce) cans tuna, drained
1 (8-ounce) package cream cheese, softened
½ cup finely shredded cheddar cheese
2 tablespoons diced onions
Prepared yellow mustard

Direction:

1 Preheat the Salter air fryer to 400 degrees Fahrenheit.
2 Make the burgers: In a large bowl, thoroughly combine the tuna, cream cheese, cheddar cheese, onions, mustard, and egg. The pork dust should be placed in a small basin.
3 Make twelve 1.5-inch balls from the tuna mixture. Roll the balls in the pork dust and form a thick crust with your palms around each ball. Flatten the balls to a thickness of half an inch.
4 Working in batches to minimize congestion, arrange the patties with room between them in the air fryer basket. Cook for eight minutes, or until golden brown and crisp, turning once. If preferred, garnish the croquettes with fresh dill and serve with cherry tomatoes, mayonnaise, and mustard on the side.
5 Refrigerate leftovers in an airtight jar for up to four days. Reheat in a preheated air fryer at 400 degrees Fahrenheit for approximately three minutes.

Coconut Shrimp

PREP TIME: 15 MINUTES • COOKING TIME: 5 MINUTES • TOTAL COOKING TIME: 20 MINUTES • SERVES: 4

Ingredients

⅔ cup cornstarch
⅔ cup sweetened coconut
1 cup panko bread crumbs
1pound uncooked large shrimp, thawed if frozen, deveined and shelled
1 (8-ounce) can crushed pineapple

½ cup sour cream
¼ cup pineapple preserves
2 egg whites
Olive oil for misting

Direction:

1. The crushed pineapple should be properly drained, saving the juice. In a small bowl, thoroughly combine the pineapple, sour cream, and preserves. Set aside. Beat the egg whites with 2 tablespoons of the reserved pineapple liquid in a small basin. The cornstarch should be placed on a plate. Combine the bread crumbs and coconut on a separate plate. The shrimp are dunked in cornstarch, shook off, then dipped in the egg white mixture, and then the coconut mixture. Place the shrimp in the basket of the Salter air fryer and spritz them with oil.
2. Air-fry the shrimp for 5 to 7 minutes, or until they are golden and crisp.

APPETIZERS

Bacon-Wrapped Pickle Spears

PREP TIME: 10 MINUTES • COOKING TIME: 8 MINUTES • TOTAL COOKING TIME: 18 MINUTES •SERVES: 4

Ingredients

8 to 12 slices bacon
¼ cup (2 ounces) cream cheese, softened
¼ cup shredded mozzarella cheese
8 dill pickle spears
½ cup ranch dressing

Direction

1. The bacon should be placed on a flat surface. Combine the cream cheese and mozzarella in a medium bowl. Stir until well blended. Spread the cheese mixture over the bacon strips.
2. Place a pickle spear on a bacon slice and roll the bacon around the pickle in a spiral, ensuring the pickle is well covered. (You may need to use more than one slice of bacon per pickle to fully cover the spear.) To ensure the bacon stays in place, tuck in the ends. Repeat to wrap all the pickles.
3. Place the wrapped pickles in the Salter air fryer basket in a single layer. Set the Salter air fryer to 400°F for 8 minutes, or until the bacon is cooked through and crisp on the edges.
4. Serve the pickle spears with ranch dressing on the side.

Buffalo Cauliflower

PREP TIME: 5 MINUTES • COOKING TIME: 11 MINUTES • TOTAL COOKING TIME: 16 MINUTES
SERVES: 4

Ingredients

¼ cup hot sauce
¼ cup powdered Parmesan cheese
2 tablespoons unsalted butter, melted
1 small head cauliflower, cut into 1-inch bites
Blue Cheese Dressing, for serving

Blue Cheese Dressing

PREP TIME: 20 MINUTES • COOKING TIME: 30 MINUTES
• TOTAL COOKING TIME: 50 MINUTES
SERVES: 2 CUPS
Ingredients

1 ½ tablespoons Swerve confectioners'-style sweetener or equivalent amount of liquid or powdered sweetener
1 tablespoon MCT oil
8 ounces crumbled blue cheese, plus more if desired for a chunky texture
¼ cup beef bone broth
¼ cup full-fat sour cream
¼ cup red wine vinegar or coconut vinegar
1 clove garlic, peeled

Direction

1. Use a food processor to puree all of the ingredients until uniform. Place into a jar. If preferred, toss in extra bits of blue cheese. The shelf life is five days if refrigerated. Preheat the Salter air fryer to 400 degrees Fahrenheit. Spray avocado oil on a baking dish that will fit in your air fryer.
2. Stir together the spicy sauce, Parmesan cheese, and butter in a large basin. Blend in the cauliflower so that it is completely covered in the sauce.
3. Place the cauliflower that has been coated in a baking dish. 11 minutes in the air fryer, stirring halfway through. To accompany with blue cheese dressing.
4. Refrigerate leftovers in an airtight jar for up to four days. To reheat, place in an oven that has been preheated to 400 degrees Fahrenheit and leave for three minutes, or until crisp and cooked through.

Ranch Roasted Chickpeas

PREP TIME: 4 MINUTES • COOKING TIME: 10 MINUTES
• TOTAL COOKING TIME: 14 MINUTES • SERVES: 4

Ingredients

1 (15-ounce) can chickpeas, drained and rinsed
1 tablespoon olive oil
3 tablespoons ranch seasoning mix
1 teaspoon salt
2 tablespoons freshly squeezed lemon juice

Direction

1 Spray the basket of the Salter air fryer with olive oil.
2 Using paper towels, thoroughly dry the chickpeas. In a medium bowl, combine the chickpeas, oil, spice blend, salt, and lemon juice. Spread the chickpeas in a single layer in the basket of the Salter air fryer. (It may be necessary to cook the chickpeas in multiple batches.)
3 Set the Salter AF's temperature to 350 degrees Fahrenheit. Set the timer for four minutes and roast. Remove the drawer and vigorously shake the chickpeas to redistribute them so they cook evenly. Reset the timer and continue roasting for six minutes. When the time is up, remove the basket from the Salter air fryer's drawer and transfer the chickpeas to a bowl. If desired, season with more salt. Enjoy!

Caramelized Onion Dip

PREP TIME:5 MINUTES •COOKING TIME: 30 MINUTES
•TOTAL COOKING TIME: 2 HOUR 35 MINUTES • SERVES: 8-10
Ingredients

1 medium yellow onion, halved and thinly sliced
¼ teaspoon kosher salt, plus additional for seasoning
4 ounces cream cheese, softened
Black pepper
½ cup sour cream
¼ teaspoon onion powder
1 tablespoon chopped fresh chives
1 tablespoon butter
Thick-cut potato chips or vegetable chips

Direction

1. Place the butter in a heat-resistant 6-by-3-inch circular pan. Place the pan in the air fryer's basket.
2. Adjust the temperature to 200 degrees Fahrenheit for one minute, or until the butter has melted. Salt and onions should be added to the pan. Adjust the temperature of the Salter air fryer to 200 degrees Fahrenheit for 15 minutes, or until the onions have softened. Adjust the temperature of the Salter air fryer to 375 degrees Fahrenheit for 15 minutes, until the onions are a deep golden brown, stirring two or three times while cooking. Allow to cool thoroughly. In a medium bowl, combine the sautéed onions, cream cheese, sour cream, onion powder, and chives. Salt and pepper are used as spices. Cover and chill for two hours to allow the flavors to combine. Serve the dip with vegetable or potato chips.

Homemade Air Fryer Roasted Mixed Nuts

PREP TIME: 5 MINUTES • COOKING TIME: 20 MINUTES

• TOTAL COOKING TIME: 25 MINUTES • SERVES: 6

Ingredients

2 cups mixed nuts (walnuts, pecans, and/or almonds)
2 tablespoons egg white
1 teaspoon ground cinnamon
2 tablespoons sugar
1 teaspoon paprika

Direction

1. Spray olive oil onto the Salter air fryer basket and preheat the fryer to 300 degrees Fahrenheit. Combine the nuts, egg white, cinnamon, sugar, and paprika in a small mixing dish until the nuts are equally coated.
2. Set the timer for 10 minutes, place the nuts in the oiled air fryer basket, and roast the nuts. Remove the drawer after 10 minutes and shake the basket to spread the nuts so that they roast evenly. Reset the timer and roast for a further 10 minutes. To serve, take the basket from the drawer and pour the nuts into a bowl.

Ranch Kale Chips

PREP TIME: 5 MINUTES • COOKING TIME: 10 MINUTES
• TOTAL COOKING TIME: 15 MINUTES • SERVES: 8 CUPS

Ingredients

½ teaspoon dried chives
½ teaspoon dried dill weed
½ teaspoon dried parsley
¼ teaspoon garlic powder
¼ teaspoon onion powder
⅛ teaspoon fine sea salt
⅛ teaspoon ground black pepper
2 large bunches kale

Direction

1 Spray avocado oil on the Salter air fryer basket. Preheat the Salter air fryer at 360 degrees Fahrenheit.
2 In a small bowl, mix together the spices, salt, and pepper.
3 Wash the kale and pat it dry thoroughly. Remove the thick inner stems with a sharp knife, then spritz the leaves with avocado oil and sprinkle them with the seasoning blend.
4 Place the kale leaves in a single layer in the air fryer and cook for 10 minutes, shaking and flipping the chips halfway through cooking. Place the baked chips on a baking pan to cool and get crisp. Proceed with the remaining kale. If wanted, sprinkle the cooled chips with salt before serving.
5 If stored in an airtight container at room temperature for up to one week, kale chips are best consumed within three days.

Cheese Drops

PREP TIME: 15 MINUTES • COOKING TIME: 10 MINUTES • TOTAL COOKING TIME: 25 MINUTES • SERVES: 4

Ingredients

¾ cup all-purpose flour
½ teaspoon kosher salt
¼ teaspoon cayenne pepper
¼ teaspoon smoked paprika
¼ teaspoon black pepper
Dash garlic powder (optional)
¼ cup butter, softened
1 cup shredded sharp cheddar cheese, at room temperature
Olive oil spray

Direction

1. In a small bowl, combine the flour, salt, cayenne, paprika, pepper, and garlic powder, if using. Butter and cheese are thoroughly combined in a food processor until smooth. Process the dough until it is well-combined, smooth, and no longer sticky after the addition of the seasoned flour. (Alternatively, prepare the dough in a stand mixer with a paddle attachment: (Beat the butter and cheese until smooth on medium speed, then add the seasoned flour and beat until smooth on low speed.)
2. Divide the dough into 32 pieces of equal size. On a floured surface, shape each part into a tiny ball.
3. Spray oil on the basket of the Salter air fryer. Place 16 cheese drops in the basket. Set the Salter air fryer to 325 degrees Fahrenheit for 10 minutes, or until the drops begin to brown. Place on a wire rack. Check the remaining dough for doneness after 8 minutes. Cool the cheese drops to room temperature on a wire rack. Store in an airtight container for up to one or two days, or until serving.

Onion Pakoras

PREP TIME: 5 MINUTES
• COOKING TIME: 10 MINUTES • TOTAL COOKING TIME: 45 MINUTES • SERVES: 4

Ingredients

2 medium yellow or white onions, sliced
½ cup chopped fresh cilantro
2 tablespoons vegetable oil
1 tablespoon chickpea flour
1 tablespoon rice flour
1 teaspoon ground turmeric
1 teaspoon cumin seeds

1 teaspoon kosher salt
½ teaspoon cayenne pepper
Vegetable oil spray

Direction

1. In a large bowl, mix together the onions, cilantro, oil, chickpea flour, rice flour, turmeric, cumin seeds, salt, and cayenne pepper. Stir to blend. Cover and allow to stand for 30 minutes to 24 hours. (This permits the onions to produce a batter by releasing moisture.) Mix carefully before use. Spray the basket of the Salter air fryer liberally with vegetable oil spray. Place six heaping tablespoons of the remaining batter into the basket.
2. 8 minutes at 350 degrees Fahrenheit and 350 degrees Fahrenheit. Turn the pakoras over carefully and spritz with oil spray. Adjust the timer on the Salter air fryer to 2 minutes, or until the batter is thoroughly cooked and crisp. Repeat with the remaining batter to make six more pakoras, then check for doneness after six minutes. Serve warm.

Lebanese Muhammara

PREP TIME: 15 MINUTES • COOKING TIME: 15 MINUTES • TOTAL COOKING TIME: 30 MINUTES • SERVES: 6

Ingredients

large red bell peppers
¼ cup plus 2 tablespoons olive oil
1 cup walnut halves
1 tablespoon agave nectar or honey
1 teaspoon fresh lemon juice
1 teaspoon ground cumin
1 teaspoon kosher salt
1 teaspoon red pepper flakes
Raw vegetables (such as cucumber, carrots, zucchini slices, or cauliflower) or toasted pita 2 chips, for serving

Direction

1 The peppers should then be placed in the air fryer basket and drizzled with 2 tablespoons of olive oil. Set the Salter air fryer to 400 degrees Fahrenheit for 10 minutes.

2 Add the walnuts to the basket so that they surround the peppers. Set the air fryer to 400 degrees Fahrenheit for 5 minutes. Remove the peppers and place them in a resealable plastic bag for 5 to 10 minutes. Place the walnuts on a plate to cool.

3 In a food processor, combine the softened peppers, walnuts, agave, lemon juice, cumin, salt, and 12 tsp of the pepper flakes until smooth. Transfer the dip to a serving bowl and create a well in the center. Pour the remaining 1/4 cup of olive oil into the crater. Use the remaining pepper flakes to decorate the dip.

4. Serve alongside grilled veggies or pita chips.

Easy Tomato And Basil Bruschetta

PREP TIME: 5 MINUTES • COOKING TIME: 3 MINUTES • TOTAL COOKING TIME: 8 MINUTES • SERVES: 6

Ingredients

¼ cup shredded Parmesan cheese
1 tablespoon minced garlic
1 tablespoon balsamic vinegar
1 teaspoon olive oil
1 teaspoon salt
1 teaspoon freshly ground black pepper
4 tomatoes, diced
⅓ cup fresh basil, shredded
1 loaf French bread

Direction

1. In a medium bowl, combine the tomatoes and basil together.
2. Incorporate the Parmesan, garlic, vinegar, olive oil, salt, and pepper into the mixture. While preparing the bread, allow the tomato mixture to settle and marinade. Spray the basket of the Salter air fryer with olive oil. The bread is sliced to a thickness of 1 inch. Place the slices in a single layer in the oiled basket of the Salter air fryer. Olive oil is sprayed on the bread.
3. Set the Salter AF's temperature to 250 degrees Fahrenheit. Set the timer for three minutes and toast the bread.
4. Using tongs, remove the bread from the air fryer and spread one tablespoon of the bruschetta topping on each piece.

Crispy Nacho Avocado Fries

PREP TIME: 10 MINUTES • COOKING TIME: 15 MINUTES • TOTAL COOKING TIME: 25 MINUTES • SERVES: 6

Ingredients

3 firm, barely ripe avocados, halved, peeled, and pitted
2 cups pork dust (or powdered Parmesan cheese for vegetarian)
2 teaspoons fine sea salt
2 teaspoons ground black pepper
2 teaspoons ground cumin
1 teaspoon chili powder
1 teaspoon paprika
½ teaspoon garlic powder
½ teaspoon onion powder

2 large eggs
Salsa, for serving (optional)
Fresh chopped cilantro leaves, for garnish (optional)

Direction

1. Spray avocado oil on the Salter air fryer basket. Preheat the Salter air fryer to 400 degrees Fahrenheit.
2. The avocados are sliced into french fry shapes.
3. In a bowl, combine the pork dust, salt, pepper, and spices.
4. In a small basin, beat the eggs separately.
5. The avocado fries are dipped in beaten eggs, shaken to remove excess, and then dipped in the pork dust mixture. Apply the breading to each fry using your hands.
6. Spray the fries with avocado oil and arrange them in a single layer in the basket of the Salter air fryer, leaving room in between. Work in batches if there are too many fries to fit in a single layer.
7. 13 to 15 minutes in the air fryer, turning after 5 minutes, until golden brown.
8. If preferred, serve with salsa and sprinkle with freshly cut cilantro. Freshest served.
9. Refrigerate leftovers in an airtight jar for up to five days. Reheat at 400 degrees Fahrenheit for three minutes in an air fryer that has been preheated.

Seasoned Sausage Rolls
PREP TIME: 5 MINUTES • COOKING TIME: 5 MINUTES
• TOTAL COOKING TIME: 10 MINUTES • SERVES: 6
Ingredients

1 (8-ounce) package crescent roll dough
2 tablespoons sesame seeds
1 ½ teaspoons poppy seeds
1 ½ teaspoons dried minced onion
1 teaspoon salt
1 teaspoon dried minced garlic
1 (12-ounce) package mini smoked sausages (cocktail franks)

Direction

1. TO PREPARE THE SAUCE: Combine the sesame seeds, poppy seeds, onion, salt, and garlic in a small bowl and put aside.
2. TO PREPARE SAUSAGES Spray olive oil onto the basket of the Salter air fryer. Unwrap the crescent dough and set it on a cutting board. Separate the dough at the locations of the perforations. Using a pizza cutter or a sharp knife, quarter each dough triangle. After being drained, the sausages should be dried with a paper towel. Each sausage is wrapped in a piece of dough. Sprinkle each bun with spice. Place the seasoned sausage rolls in a single layer in the oiled basket of the Salter air fryer.
3. Adjust the temperature of the Salter AF to 330 degrees Fahrenheit. Set a five-minute timer. Remove the sausages from the air fryer using tongs and lay them on a platter. Steps 6 through 8 must be repeated with the second batch.

Homemade Air Fryer Pita Chips

PREP TIME: 5 MINUTES • COOKING TIME: 6 MINUTES • TOTAL COOKING TIME: 11 MINUTES • SERVES: 4

Ingredients

2 pieces whole wheat pita bread
3 tablespoons olive oil
1 teaspoon freshly squeezed lemon juice
1 teaspoon salt
1 teaspoon dried basil
1 teaspoon garlic powder

Direction

1. Spray the basket of the Salter air fryer with olive oil. Using kitchen scissors or a pizza cutter, cut the pita bread into small wedges. Add the wedges, olive oil, lemon juice, salt, dried basil, and garlic powder to a small mixing bowl. Mix thoroughly to coat each wedge. Place the pita wedges in an even layer in the Salter air fryer's oiled basket, taking care not to crowd them.
2. Set the Salter AF's temperature to 350 degrees Fahrenheit. Set the timer for 6 minutes and bake. Remove the drawer and jiggle the basket of pita chips every 2 minutes or so to achieve uniform cooking. Serve with your favorite dipping sauce or as a refreshing snack on its own.

Bacon-Wrapped Pickle Poppers

PREP TIME: 10 MINUTES • COOKING TIME: 10 MINUTES • TOTAL COOKING TIME: 20 MINUTES • SERVES: 24 POPPERS

Ingredients

12 medium dill pickles
1 (8-ounce) package cream cheese, softened
1 cup shredded sharp cheddar cheese
12 slices bacon or beef bacon, sliced in half lengthwise
Ranch Dressing or Blue Cheese Dressing, for serving (optional)

Direction

1. Spray avocado oil on the Salter air fryer basket. Adjust the temperature of the Salter air fryer to 400 degrees Fahrenheit. Cut the dill pickles in half along their length and use a spoon to remove the interiors. The cream cheese and cheddar cheese should be thoroughly mixed in a small bowl. In equal amounts, distribute the cream cheese mixture into the hollowed-out centers of the pickles. Each pickle is wrapped with bacon and secured with a toothpick.
2. Seam side down, place the bacon-wrapped pickles in the basket of the Salter air fryer and cook for 8 to 10 minutes, flipping the pickles halfway through, until the bacon is crispy. If desired, serve warm with ranch or blue cheese dressing.
3. Freshest ingredients served. Refrigerate leftovers for up to five days in an airtight container.

Reheat at 400 degrees Fahrenheit for three minutes in an air fryer that has been preheated.

Doro Wat Wings

PREP TIME: 5 MINUTES • COOKING TIME: 32 MINUTES • TOTAL COOKING TIME: 37 MINUTES •SERVES: 1 DOZEN WINGS

Ingredients

2 teaspoons berbere spice
1 teaspoon fine sea salt
2 hard-boiled eggs
½ teaspoon fine sea salt
¼ teaspoon berbere spice
1 dozen chicken wings or drummies
1 tablespoon coconut oil or bacon fat, melted
¼ teaspoon dried chives

Direction

1. Spray avocado oil on the Salter air fryer basket. Preheat the Salter air fryer to 380 °F.
2. The wings of chicken are placed in a large basin. Pour the oil over the vegetables and flip to evenly coat. The chicken is coated with salt and berbere on all sides.
3. Air-fry the chicken wings for 25 minutes, turning after 15 minutes.
4. After 25 minutes, increase the temperature to 400 degrees Fahrenheit and continue cooking for an additional 6 to 7 minutes, or until the skin is golden brown and crisp.
5. While the chicken is cooking, if desired, prepare the eggs: The eggs should be peeled, halved, and seasoned with salt, berbere, and dried chives. Serve the chicken and eggs together.

Bourbon Chicken Wings

PREP TIME: 10 MINUTES • COOKING TIME: 32 MINUTES • TOTAL COOKING TIME: 42 MINUTES • SERVES: 8

Ingredients

½ teaspoon fine sea salt
½ cup chicken broth
⅓ cup Swerve confectioners'-style sweetener or equivalent amount of liquid or powdered sweetener
1 clove garlic, smashed to a paste
FOR GARNISH (OPTIONAL):
Chopped green onions
¼ cup tomato sauce
¼ cup wheat-free tamari
1 tablespoon apple cider vinegar
¾ teaspoon red pepper flakes
¼ teaspoon grated fresh ginger

2 pounds chicken wings or drummies
Sesame seeds

Direction

1. Spray avocado oil on the basket of the Salter air fryer. Preheat the Salter air fryer to 380 degrees Fahrenheit.
2. Salt all sides of the chicken wings before placing them in the air fryer.
3. Cook for 25 minutes, flipping the dish every 15 minutes. After 25 minutes, raise the temperature to 400 degrees Fahrenheit and cook for an additional 6 to 7 minutes, until the skin is golden and crisp.

SNACKS & DESSERTS

Perfect Cinnamon Toast

PREP TIME: 10 MINUTES • COOKING TIME: 5 MINUTES • TOTAL COOKING TIME: 15 MINUTES • *SERVES: 6*

Ingredients

1 ½ tsp. vanilla extract
1 ½ tsp. cinnamon
½ C. sweetener of choice
1 C. coconut oil
2 tsp. pepper
12 slices whole wheat bread

Direction:

1. Combine coconut oil and sugar until the sugar is completely dissolved. Except for the bread, thoroughly combine the remaining ingredients. Spread mixture on bread, covering the entire surface.
2. Place coated bread slices in the Air fryer.
3. Cook 5 minutes at 400 degrees. Remove and make a diagonal cut. Enjoy.

Easy Baked Chocolate Mug Cake

PREP TIME: 5 MINUTES • COOKING TIME: 15 MINUTES • TOTAL COOKING TIME: 20 MINUTES • *SERVES: 3*

Ingredients

½ cup cocoa powder
½ cup stevia powder
1 cup coconut cream
1 package cream cheese, room temperature
1 tablespoon vanilla extract
4 tablespoons butter

Direction:

1. The Salter air fryer should be preheated for five minutes. In a bowl, combine all of the ingredients. Combine all ingredients with a hand mixer until frothy. Transfer to greased mugs. The mugs should be placed in the fryer basket.
2. Bake for 15 minutes at 350°F.
3. Place in the refrigerator before serving to chill.

Easy Chocolate-Frosted Doughnuts

PREP TIME: 5 MINUTES • COOKING TIME: 5 MINUTES • TOTAL COOKING TIME: 10 MINUTES • *SERVES: 6*

Ingredients

1 (16.3-ounce / 8-count) package refrigerated biscuit dough
¾ cup powdered sugar
¼ cup unsweetened cocoa powder
¼ cup milk

Direction:

2 Spray the basket of the Salter air fryer with olive oil.
3 On a cutting board, unroll the biscuit dough and separate the biscuits.
4 Using a 1-inch-diameter biscuit or cookie cutter, remove the center of each biscuit.
5 Insert the donuts into the air fryer. (You may need to fry doughnuts in multiple batches.)
6 Set the Salter AF's temperature to 330 degrees Fahrenheit. Set the timer for 5 minutes and bake.
7 Remove the doughnuts from the air fryer with tongs and allow them to cool before coating.
8 In the interim, whisk together the powdered sugar, unsweetened cocoa powder, and milk in a small mixing bowl.
9 Use a knife to spread the icing uniformly around the doughnuts after dipping them in the glaze.

Allow the glaze to harden before serving.

Air Fryer Homemade Pumpkin Fritters

PREP TIME: 5 MINUTES • COOKING TIME: 9 MINUTES • TOTAL COOKING TIME: 14 MINUTES • *SERVES: 8 FRITTERS*

Ingredients

½ cup chopped pecans
¼ cup pumpkin purée
¼ cup sugar
1 teaspoon pumpkin pie spice
1 cup powdered sugar
2 tablespoons milk (plus more to thin the glaze, if necessary)
1 teaspoon pumpkin pie spice
1 tablespoon pumpkin purée
1 (16.3-ounce, 8-count) package refrigerated biscuit dough
2 tablespoons unsalted butter, melted

Direction:

1 TO MAKE THE FRENCH FRIES. Spray the basket of the Salter air fryer with olive oil, or spray a baking sheet sized for the air fryer with olive oil or cooking spray. The biscuit

dough was spread out on a cutting board. Cut each cookie into eight pieces. Once all the pieces have been cut, place them in a medium-sized mixing bowl. Toss the biscuit crumbs with the pecans, pumpkin, sugar, and pumpkin pie spice until completely incorporated. Form the dough into eight equal mounds. Drizzle butter over each of the fritters.

2. Place the fritters directly in the oiled basket of the air fryer, or on a baking sheet oiled and placed in the air fryer basket. Set the Salter AF's temperature to 330 degrees Fahrenheit. Set the timer for 7 minutes and bake.
3. Determine whether the fritters are done. The dough should be fully baked and firm to the touch. If not, cook for an additional one to two minutes. Using tongs, remove the fritters from the air fryer. Ten minutes must pass before applying the glaze.

TO MAKE THE GLAZE

In a small mixing bowl, thoroughly combine the powdered sugar, pumpkin, pumpkin pie spice, and milk. If it resembles frosting, it is excessively thick. It should have a pourable consistency and adhere to a spoon.

The glaze is drizzled over the fritters.

Angel Food Cake

PREP TIME: 5 MINUTES • COOKING TIME: 30 MINUTES • TOTAL COOKING TIME: 35 MINUTES • *SERVES: 12*

Ingredients

1 cup powdered erythritol
1 teaspoon strawberry extract
12 egg whites
2 teaspoons cream of tartar
¼ cup butter, melted
A pinch of salt

Direction:

1. The Salter air fryer should be preheated for five minutes.
2. Combining egg whites and cream of tartar is required. Whisk with a hand mixer until the mixture is white and frothy.
3. Add the remaining ingredients, excluding the butter, and whisk for an additional minute.
4. Pour into a dish that is oven-safe.
5. Place in the basket of the Salter air fryer and cook at 400°F for 30 minutes, or until a toothpick inserted in the center comes out clean. Once cool, drizzle with melted butter.

Air Fryer Homemade Chocolate Chip Cookies

PREP TIME: 5 MINUTES • COOKING TIME: 5 MINUTES • TOTAL COOKING TIME: 10 MINUTES • *SERVES: 25 COOKIES*

Ingredients

1 cup (2 sticks) unsalted butter, at room temperature
1 cup granulated sugar
1 cup brown sugar
2 large eggs
½ teaspoon vanilla extract
1 teaspoon baking soda
½ teaspoon salt
3 cups all-purpose flour
2 cups chocolate chips

Direction:

1. Spray an air fryer-sized baking sheet with cooking spray.
2. Cream together the butter and both sugars in a large bowl. Mix the flour, eggs, vanilla, baking soda, and salt until thoroughly incorporated. Incorporate the chocolate chips. Utilize your hands to knead the dough until everything is thoroughly combined. Using a cookie scoop or a tablespoon, place generous spoonfuls of dough about 1 inch apart onto the baking sheet.
3. Insert the baking sheet into the air fryer. Set the Salter AF's temperature to 340 degrees Fahrenheit. Set the timer for 5 minutes and bake. When the cookies are golden brown and fully cooked, remove the baking sheet from the air fryer with silicone oven mitts and serve. If you line the basket of your Salter air fryer with cooking-sprayed air fryer parchment paper, you may cook numerous batches of cookies with minimal cleanup.

Fried Peaches

PREP TIME: 2 HOURS 10 MINUTES • COOKING TIME: 15 MINUTES • TOTAL COOKING TIME: 15 MINUTES • ***SERVES: 4***

Ingredients

4 ripe peaches (1/2 a peach = 1 serving)
1 1/2 cups flour
Salt
2 egg yolks
3/4 cups cold water
1 1/2 tablespoons olive oil
2 tablespoons brandy
4 egg whites
Cinnamon/sugar mix

Direction:

1 In a bowl, combine flour, egg yolks, and salt. Slowly combine water and brandy. Set the mixture aside for two hours, then occupy yourself for one hour and forty-five minutes.

2 Bring a big saucepan of water to a boil and score the bottom of each peach with an X. While the water is boiling, fill a second big basin with ice and water. Each peach should be boiled for

about one minute, then placed in the ice bath. Now, the peels of the peach should fall off. Beat the egg whites and mix them into the batter. Dip each peach in the mix to coat.

3. 10 minutes at 360 degrees Fahrenheit.
4. Serve peaches rolled in the cinnamon-sugar mixture on a platter.

Apple Dumplings

PREP TIME: 10 MINUTES • COOKING TIME: 25 MINUTES • TOTAL COOKING TIME: 35 MINUTES • ***SERVES: 4***

Ingredients

2 tbsp. melted coconut oil
2 puff pastry sheets
1 tbsp. brown sugar
2 tbsp. raisins
2 small apples of choice

Direction:

1. In a bowl, combine flour, egg yolks, and salt. Slowly combine water and brandy. Set the mixture aside for two hours, then occupy yourself for one hour and forty-five minutes.
2. Bring a big saucepan of water to a boil and score the bottom of each peach with an X. While the water is boiling, fill a second big basin with ice and water. Each peach should be boiled for about one minute, then placed in the ice bath. Now, the peels of the peach should fall off. Beat the egg whites and mix them into the batter. Dip each peach in the mix to coat.
3. 10 minutes at 360 degrees Fahrenheit.
4. Serve peaches rolled in the cinnamon-sugar mixture on a platter.

Air Fryer Stuffed Baked Apples

PREP TIME: 5 MINUTES • COOKING TIME: 20 MINUTES • TOTAL COOKING TIME: 15 MINUTES • ***SERVES: 4***

Ingredients

4 to 6 tablespoons raisins
4 tablespoons (½ stick) unsalted butter, melted
1 teaspoon ground cinnamon
½ teaspoon ground nutmeg
4 apples, cored but with the bottoms left intact
Vanilla ice cream, for topping
4 to 6 tablespoons chopped walnuts
Maple syrup, for topping

Direction:

1. In a small basin, mix the filling ingredients. Mix together the walnuts, raisins, melted butter, cinnamon, and nutmeg.
2. Put a quarter of the filling into each apple. Insert the apples in an air fryer-compatible pan and

place the pan within the air fryer's basket.

3. Set the temperature of the Salter AF to 350 degrees Fahrenheit. Set the timer for 20 minutes and bake the ingredients.
4. Serve with vanilla ice cream and a drizzle of maple syrup. To make baked apples with oatmeal filling, combine 1 cup of rolled oats with 1/4 cup of brown sugar.

Easy Air Fried Apple Hand Pies

PREP TIME: 5 MINUTES • COOKING TIME: 7 MINUTES • TOTAL COOKING TIME: 12 MINUTES • ***SERVES: 8 HAND PIES***

Ingredients

1 package prepared pie dough
½ cup apple pie filling
1 large egg white
1 tablespoon Wilton White Sparkling Sugar
Caramel sauce, for drizzling

Direction:

1. Spray the basket of the Salter air fryer with olive oil. Lightly flour a clean work surface. Spread out the dough on your workspace. Using a 2-inch biscuit cutter, cut eight circles out of the dough. Gather the fragments of dough, form them into a ball, and reroll them. Form biscuits from the leftover dough using the biscuit cutter. Add approximately 1 teaspoon of apple pie filling to the center of each round. Fold the dough over and use a fork to seal the edges. Sprinkle sparkling sugar over the egg white-coated surface. Place the hand pies in the air fryer's greased basket. They must be separated so that they cannot come into contact.
2. Set the temperature of the Salter AF to 350 degrees Fahrenheit. Set the timer for five minutes and bake the food. The crust should be golden brown when completion. If not done, bake for two minutes more. If desired, drizzle caramel sauce over the dish.

Apple Pie in Air Fryer

PREP TIME: 5 MINUTES • COOKING TIME: 35 MINUTES • TOTAL COOKING TIME: 40 MINUTES • ***SERVES: 4***

Ingredients

1 Pillsbury Refrigerator pie crust
1 tablespoon ground cinnamon
1 tablespoon raw sugar
2 tablespoon sugar
2 teaspoons lemon juice
½ teaspoon vanilla extract
1 beaten egg
1 large apple, chopped
1 tablespoon butter
Baking spray

Direction:

1 Spray the baking pan of the air fryer lightly with cooking spray. Spread pie crust on the bottom of the pan and up the sides. In a bowl, combine apples, vanilla, sugar, cinnamon, and lemon juice. Pour the liquid over the pie crust. The apples are covered with pieces of butter. Cover apples with leftover pie crust. Using a knife, pierce the pies' tops. On top of the crust, spread egg beaten with sugar. encase in foil

2 For 25 minutes, cook at 390 degrees Fahrenheit. Remove foil and cook at 330 degrees Fahrenheit for 10 minutes, or until the tops are golden brown. Serve with enthusiasm.

Easy Air Fryer Blueberry Pie

PREP TIME: 5 MINUTES PLUS 30 MINUTES TO THAW • COOKING TIME: 18 MINUTES • TOTAL COOKING TIME: 53 MINUTES • ***SERVES: 4-6***

Ingredients

2 (21-ounce) jars blueberry pie filling
1 teaspoon milk
2 frozen pie crusts
1 teaspoon sugar

Direction:

1 Take the pie crusts out of the freezer and let them to thaw for 30 minutes on the counter. One pie crust should be used to line the bottom of a 6-inch pie dish. Pour the pie filling into the bottom crust, then seal the sides by pushing the top and bottom crusts together. Remove any excess pie crust. Using a knife or a small cookie cutter with a beautiful shape, create holes in the top crust. Apply milk to the top crust, then sprinkle it with sugar. Place the pie in the air fryer's basket.

2 Adjust the temperature of the Salter AF to 310 degrees Fahrenheit. Set the timer for fifteen minutes, then bake.

3 After fifteen minutes, inspect the pie. If additional time is required, restart the timer and bake for three minutes more. Using silicone oven mitts, remove the pie from the air fryer and allow it to cool for 15 minutes before serving.

Air Fryer Chocolate Cake

PREP TIME: 5 MINUTES • COOKING TIME: 35 MINUTES • TOTAL COOKING TIME: 40 MINUTES • ***SERVES: 8-10***

Ingredients

½ C. unsweetened cocoa powder
2 C. almond flour
½ C. hot water
1 tsp. vanilla
¼ C. olive oil
½ C. almond milk
½ tsp. salt

¾ tsp. baking soda
¾ tsp. baking powder
1 egg
1 C. brown sugar

Direction:

1. Preheat your air fryer to a temperature of 356 degrees Fahrenheit.
2. Combine all of the dry ingredients. Then, whisk in the wet ingredients. Add hot water last.
3. The batter will be thin; do not be alarmed.
4. Inject cake batter into a pan that is suitable for frying. Cover with aluminum foil and make holes in it. Bake 35 minutes. Remove the foil and bake for 10 minutes longer.

Raspberry Cream Rol-Ups

PREP TIME: 10 MINUTES • COOKING TIME: 25 MINUTES • TOTAL COOKING TIME: 35 MINUTES • ***SERVES: 4***

Ingredients

1 cup of fresh raspberries, rinsed and patted dry
½ cup of cream cheese, softened to room temperature
¼ cup of brown sugar
¼ cup of sweetened condensed milk
1 egg
1 teaspoon of corn starch
6 spring roll wrappers
¼ cup of water

Direction:

1. Cover the Air fryer's basket with aluminum foil, leaving the edges free for air circulation. The air fryer should be preheated to 350 degrees Fahrenheit. In a mixing bowl, combine the cream cheese, brown sugar, condensed milk, cornstarch, and egg. Beat or whip until all ingredients are well incorporated, airy, and thick. Spoon equal amounts of the creamy filling into each spring roll wrapper, followed by a few raspberries on top of each part. A few drops of water are used to seal the wraps' seams after they are rolled around a creamy raspberry filling. Place each roll seam-side down in the Air fryer basket lined with aluminum foil.
2. Set the Salter air fryer's timer to 10 minutes. Shake the fryer basket's handle while frying to ensure an evenly crisped surface. After 10 minutes, when the Air fryer shuts off, the exterior of the spring rolls should be golden brown and flawless, while the filling of raspberries and cream will have cooked into a delectable fusion. Serve hot or cold, using tongs to remove.

Air Fryer Banana Cake

PREP TIME: 5 MINUTES • COOKING TIME: 30 MINUTES • TOTAL COOKING TIME: 35 MINUTES • ***SERVES: 4***

Ingredients

4 tablespoons (½ stick) unsalted butter, at room temperature
1 ripe banana, mashed
1 large egg
2 tablespoons granulated sugar
1 cup all-purpose flour
1 teaspoon ground cinnamon
1 teaspoon vanilla extract
⅓ cup brown sugar
½ teaspoon ground nutmeg

Direction:

1. Spray a Bundt pan with a diameter of 6 inches with cooking spray.
2. Brown sugar and butter are creamed together in a medium basin until light and fluffy.
3. Combine the banana and the egg. Combine the granulated sugar, flour, cinnamon powder, vanilla, and nutmeg. Spoon the batter into the pan you have prepared. Place the pan in the air fryer's basket.
4. Adjust the temperature of the Salter AF to 320 degrees Fahrenheit. Set the timer for fifteen minutes, then bake.
5. Consider the toothpick test. If there are no crumbs on the toothpick, the cake is ready. If there is cake batter on the toothpick, continue cooking and examining the cake every 5 minutes until it is done. It will likely take about 30 minutes to bake thoroughly. With silicone oven mitts, remove the Bundt pan from the air fryer. Set the pan on a cooling rack and let it to cool for approximately ten minutes. Place a plate inverted on top of the Bundt pan, as if it were a lid. Invert the plate and pan with care, and place the plate on the counter. The Bundt ring must be removed from the cake. Frost as desired.

Banana-Choco Brownies

PREP TIME: 5 MINUTES • COOKING TIME: 30 MINUTES • TOTAL COOKING TIME: 35 MINUTES • ***SERVES: 12***

Ingredients

2 teaspoons baking powder
½ teaspoon baking powder
½ teaspoon baking soda
½ teaspoon salt
1 over-ripe banana
3 large eggs
½ teaspoon stevia powder
¼ cup coconut oil
1 tablespoon vinegar

1/3 cup almond flour
2 cups almond flour
1/3 cup cocoa powder

Direction:

1. The Salter air fryer should be preheated for five minutes. In a food processor, pulse all ingredients until they are fully combined. Pour the ingredients into a baking dish compatible with an air fryer.
2. Place in the basket of the Salter air fryer and cook at 350 degrees Fahrenheit for thirty minutes, or until a toothpick inserted into the center of the food comes out clean.

Easy Air Fried Old-Fashioned Cherry Cobbler

PREP TIME: 5 MINUTES • COOKING TIME: 35 MINUTES • TOTAL COOKING TIME: 15 MINUTES • ***SERVES: 4***

Ingredients

1 cup sugar
2 tablespoons baking powder
¾ cup milk
8 tablespoons (1 stick) unsalted butter
1 cup all-purpose flour
1 (21-ounce) can cherry pie filling

Direction:

1. In a small bowl, combine the flour, sugar, and baking powder. Add milk and fully blend the ingredients. In a small microwave-safe bowl, melt the butter for approximately 45 seconds in the microwave. Spread the batter evenly over the bottom of a buttered 8-by-8-inch pan. The filling is poured over the pie dough. Do not combine; the batter will rise through the filling during cooking.
2. Adjust the temperature of the Salter AF to 320 degrees Fahrenheit. Set the timer for 20 minutes and bake the ingredients.
3. Check out the cobbler. The batter will be golden brown and completely baked when the cobbler has done baking. If not done, bake for a further 5 minutes and test again for doneness. The overall cooking time is anticipated to be between 30 and 35 minutes. Remove the meal from the air fryer and allow it to cool before serving.

Chocolate Donuts

PREP TIME: 5 MINUTES • COOKING TIME: 20 MINUTES • TOTAL COOKING TIME: 25 MINUTES • ***SERVES: 8-10***

Ingredients

(8-ounce) can jumbo biscuits
Cooking oil
Chocolate sauce, such as Hershey's

Direction:

1. Separate the dough into eight separate biscuits and place them on a flat surface. Use a small round cookie cutter or a biscuit cutter to create a hole in the center of each biscuit. You can also cut the holes with a knife.
2. Spray cooking oil onto the basket of the Salter air fryer.
3. Place four doughnuts inside the air fryer. Never stack. Oil is sprayed for cooking. Prepare yourself for four minutes.
4. Turn the doughnuts over and then open the air fryer. Cook for an additional four minutes.
5. Repeat steps 3 and 4 with the remaining four doughnuts.

While the doughnuts are still warm, spread chocolate sauce over them and enjoy.

Homemade Air Fried Fudge Brownies

PREP TIME: 5 MINUTES • COOKING TIME: 20 MINUTES • TOTAL COOKING TIME: 25 MINUTES • *SERVES: 6*

Ingredients

1 cup sugar
1 teaspoon vanilla extract
2 large eggs
½ cup all-purpose flour
½ cup cocoa powder
8 tablespoons (1 stick) unsalted butter, melted
1 teaspoon baking powder

Direction:

1 Use cooking spray or butter to oil an air fryer-compatible 6-inch baking dish. In a larger bowl, whisk together the butter, sugar, vanilla, and eggs until fully combined. Combine the flour, cocoa powder, and baking powder until smooth. Pour the batter into the prepared baking dish.

2 Set the temperature of the Salter AF to 350 degrees Fahrenheit. Set the timer for 20 minutes and bake the ingredients. Using silicon oven mitts, remove the pan from the air fryer once the middle has solidified. Allow to cool somewhat prior to serving.

Chocolate Bundt Cake

PREP TIME: 5 MINUTES • COOKING TIME: 30 MINUTES • TOTAL COOKING TIME: 35 MINUTES • *SERVES: 4*

Ingredients

2 cups sugar
¾ cup unsweetened cocoa powder
1 teaspoon baking soda

1 teaspoon baking powder
½ cup vegetable oil
1 teaspoon salt
2 teaspoons vanilla extract
2 large eggs
1 cup milk
1¾ cups all-purpose flour
1 cup hot water

Direction:

1. Spray a Bundt pan with a diameter of 6 inches with cooking spray.
2. In a large mixing bowl, combine the flour, sugar, cocoa powder, baking soda, baking powder, oil, salt, vanilla, eggs, milk, and boiling water. Place the pan containing the cake batter in the air fryer basket.
3. Adjust the temperature of the Salter AF to 330 degrees Fahrenheit. Set the timer for 20 minutes and bake the ingredients. Consider the toothpick test. If there are no crumbs on the toothpick, the cake is ready. If there is cake batter on the toothpick, continue cooking and examining the cake every 5 minutes until it is done. It will likely take about 30 minutes to bake thoroughly. With silicone oven mitts, remove the Bundt pan from the air fryer. Ten minutes later, place the pan on a cooling rack and allow it to cool. Place a platter inverted atop the Bundt pan. Invert the plate and pan with care, and place the plate on the counter. The Bundt ring must be removed from the cake.

Easy Air Fryer Donuts

PREP TIME: 5 MINUTES • COOKING TIME: 5 MINUTES • TOTAL COOKING TIME: 10 MINUTES • *SERVES: 8*

Ingredients

4 tbsp. dark brown sugar
½ - 1 tsp. cinnamon
1/3 C. granulated sweetener
3 tbsp. melted coconut oil
Pinch of allspice
1 can of biscuits

Direction:

1. Combine allspice, sugar, artificial sweetener, and cinnamon.
2. Before placing biscuits in an air fryer, remove them from the can and create holes in their centers with a round cookie cutter.
3. Cook 5 minutes at 350 degrees. Using a paintbrush, coat each cookie with melted coconut oil while it is baked, and then dip each biscuit into the sugar mixture.
4. Serve warm.

Little French Fudge Cakes

PREP TIME: 10 MINUTES • COOKING TIME: 25 MINUTES • TOTAL COOKING TIME: 35 MINUTES • *SERVES: 12 CAKES*

Ingredients

2 tablespoons Swerve confectioners'-style sweetener or liquid sweetener
½ cup chopped walnuts or pecans, for garnish (optional)
½ cup Swerve confectioners'-style sweetener
½ cup (1 stick) unsalted butter, melted
4 ounces cream cheese (½ cup) softened
3 tablespoons unsweetened, unflavored almond milk or heavy cream
3 tablespoons unsalted butter
1 teaspoon baking soda
½ teaspoon fine sea salt
6 large eggs
1 cup Swerve confectioners'-style sweetener
1½ cups canned pumpkin puree
3 tablespoons brewed decaf espresso or other strong brewed decaf coffee
3 tablespoons unsalted butter, melted but not hot
2 tablespoons unsweetened cocoa powder
¼ cup unsweetened, unflavored almond milk
3 cups blanched almond flour
¾ cup unsweetened cocoa powder
1 teaspoon vanilla extract

Direction:

1. Heat the Salter air fryer to 350 degrees Fahrenheit before use. Coconut oil should be applied to two tiny Bundt pans.
2. In a larger bowl, whisk together the flour, cocoa powder, baking soda, and salt until homogeneous.
3. In a large bowl, beat the eggs and sugar with a hand mixer for 2 to 3 minutes, until light and fluffy. Mix the pumpkin puree, espresso, melted butter, and vanilla essence together.
4. Whisk the wet ingredients into the dry ingredients until just combined.
5. Pour two-thirds of the batter into the prepared baking pans.
6. Twenty to twenty-five minutes in the air fryer, or until a toothpick inserted into the center of the cake comes out clean. Allow the cakes to cool completely in their pans before removing them. Make the frosting: Combine the sweetener, melted butter, and cream cheese in a large bowl. Stir the almond milk into the mixture well.
7. To prepare the chocolate drizzle, properly combine the melted butter, sugar, and cocoa powder in a small bowl. Incorporate the almond milk while stirring to thin the mixture. After the cakes have cooled, dip the tops of each cake into the frosting before drizzling chocolate over the frosted cakes. If desired, top the cakes with chopped nuts.
8. Refrigerate leftovers for up to four days in an airtight container, or freeze them for up to one month.

Chocolate Soufflé for Two

PREP TIME: 5 MINUTES • COOKING TIME: 14 MINUTES • TOTAL COOKING TIME: 19 MINUTES • ***SERVES: 2***

Ingredients

½ tsp. vanilla
3 tbsp. sweetener
2 separated eggs
¼ C. melted coconut oil
2 tbsp. almond flour
3 ounces of semi-sweet chocolate, chopped

Direction:

1. Sugar and coconut oil are spread onto ramekins.
2. Chocolate and coconut oil are heated together.
3. Beat egg yolks well, adding vanilla and sweetener. Incorporate the flour and ensure that no lumps remain. The fryer should be heated to 330 degrees Fahrenheit. Whisk egg whites until they form firm peaks, then gently fold them into the chocolate mixture. Inject batter into ramekins before placing them in a fryer.
4. Cook 14 minutes. Served dusted with powdered sugar.

Fried Bananas with Chocolate Sauce

PREP TIME: 10 MINUTES • COOKING TIME: 10 MINUTES • TOTAL COOKING TIME: 20 MINUTES • ***SERVES: 2***

Ingredients

1 large egg
¼ cup cornstarch
¼ cup plain bread crumbs
3 bananas, halved crosswise
Cooking oil
Chocolate sauce

Direction:

1. In a small bowl, beat the egg. In a separate bowl, combine the cornstarch and water. Place the crumbs in the final basin. The bananas are dipped in cornstarch, followed by egg, and finally bread crumbs.
2. Spray cooking oil onto the basket of the Salter air fryer. The bananas are sprayed with frying oil and placed in a basket.
3. Prepare for 5 minutes. Take the bananas out of the air fryer and flip them. Continue cooking for an additional two minutes. Put the bananas on a plate.
4. Pour the chocolate sauce over the bananas to serve.
5. You can make your own chocolate sauce using 2 tablespoons of milk and 1/4 cup chocolate chips. Over medium heat, bring a pot to a boil. Stir the milk into the mixture for one to two

minutes. Utilize chocolate chips. Stir for two minutes, or until the chocolate has melted.

Flourless Cream-Filled Mini Cakes

PREP TIME: 10 MINUTES • COOKING TIME: 10 MINUTES • TOTAL COOKING TIME: 20 MINUTES • ***SERVES: 8***

Ingredients

4 ounces unsweetened chocolate, chopped
¾ cup Swerve confectioners'-style sweetener or equivalent amount of powdered sweetener
3 large eggs
1 (8-ounce) package cream cheese softened
¼ cup Swerve confectioners'-style sweetener
Whipped cream
½ cup (1 stick) unsalted butter
Raspberries

Direction:

1 Preheat the Salter air fryer to 375 degrees Fahrenheit. Grease eight 4-ounce ramekins. Prepare the baking mix by In a saucepan, whisk the butter and chocolate constantly over low heat until the chocolate is completely melted. Remove yourself from the heat.
2 With a hand mixer on low speed, combine the sweetener and eggs. Set aside.
3 Prepare the filling by following these steps: In a medium bowl, thoroughly combine the cream cheese and sugar. If desired, taste and add additional sugar. Butter each ramekin and fill them halfway with the chocolate mixture. Add 1 spoonful of the filling to each ramekin on top of the chocolate mixture.
4 Ten minutes, or until the exterior is firm and the interior is warm and soft, place the ramekins in the air fryer. Allow it to cool completely, then, if desired, garnish with whipped cream and raspberries.

Chocolaty Banana Muffins

PREP TIME: 5 MINUTES • COOKING TIME: 25 MINUTES • TOTAL COOKING TIME: 35 MINUTES • ***SERVES: 12***

Ingredients

¾ cup plain flour
¼ cup cocoa powder
¼ teaspoon baking powder
1 teaspoon baking soda
¼ teaspoon salt
2 large bananas, peeled and mashed
1 cup sugar
1/3 cup canola oil
1 egg

½ teaspoon vanilla essence
¾ cup whole wheat flour
1 cup mini chocolate chips

Direction:

1 In a large bowl, combine flour, cocoa powder, baking powder, baking soda, and salt. Blend bananas, sugar, oil, egg, and vanilla essence in a separate bowl. Combine the flour mixture and egg mixture slowly until just combined. Utilize chocolate chips. The air fryer should be preheated to 345 degrees Fahrenheit. Prepare twelve muffin cups with cooking spray.

2 Bake for 20 to 25 minutes, or until a toothpick inserted in the center of the muffins comes out clean. Remove the muffin tins from the Air fryer and place them on a cooling rack for 10 minutes. Place on a wire rack for complete cooling before serving.

Halle Berries-and-Cream Cobbler

PREP TIME: 10 MINUTES • COOKING TIME: 25 MINUTES • TOTAL COOKING TIME: 35 MINUTES • ***SERVES: 4***

Ingredients

2 ounces cream cheese (¼ cup), softened
1 Tablespoon Swerve confectioners'-style sweetener or liquid sweetener
1 tablespoon unsweetened, unflavored almond milk or heavy cream
Fresh raspberries or strawberries, for garnish
12 ounces cream cheese (1½ cups), softened
1 large egg
¾ cup Swerve confectioners'-style sweetener
½ teaspoon vanilla extract
¼ teaspoon fine sea salt
3 large egg whites
¾ cup blanched almond flour
1 teaspoon baking powder
2½ tablespoons very cold unsalted butter, cut into pieces
¼ teaspoon fine sea salt
1 cup sliced fresh raspberries or strawberries

Direction:

1 Adjust the temperature of the Salter air fryer to 400 degrees Fahrenheit. Coat a seven-inch pie dish with butter.

2 In a large mixing bowl, thoroughly combine the cream cheese, egg, and sweetener with a hand mixer. Add vanilla essence and salt to the mixture. Using a rubber spatula, incorporate the raspberries into the mixture in a gentle manner. Pour the mixture into the baking dish that has been prepared and reserve. Prepare the biscuits: Place the egg whites in a medium-sized mixing dish or the bowl of a stand mixer. Using a hand mixer or stand mixer, whip the egg whites until they are extremely airy and stiff. In a separate, similar-sized bowl, combine the almond flour and baking powder. Cut the butter into little pieces and slowly stir in

the salt to maintain the butter's texture. Gently incorporate the almond flour mixture into the egg whites. Using a large spoon or ice cream scoop, shape the dough into 2-inch-wide biscuits while ensuring the butter remains in distinct clumps. Place the biscuit on top of the raspberry mixture in the pan. Repeat with the remaining dough to create a total of four biscuits.

3 Reduce the temperature to 325 degrees Fahrenheit and bake the biscuits for an additional 17 to 20 minutes, or until golden brown. While the cobbler is baking, make the frosting: Place the cream cheese in a small bowl and, using a spoon, break it up. Stir in the sugar substitute. Stir almond milk until completely combined. Add more almond milk if you prefer a frosting with a thinner consistency. Pour the frosting over the cobbler after taking it from the air fryer and letting it to cool. Use fresh raspberries as an embellishment.

4 Keep leftovers in an airtight jar in the refrigerator for up to three days. Reheat the cobbler in a hot air fryer at 350 degrees Fahrenheit for three minutes, or until heated thoroughly.

Apple Hand Pies

PREP TIME: 5 MINUTES • COOKING TIME: 8 MINUTES • TOTAL COOKING TIME: 13 MINUTES • ***SERVES: 6***

Ingredients

15-ounces no-sugar-added apple pie filling
1 store-bought crust

Direction:

1 Spread out pie crust and cut into equal-sized squares.

2 Fill each square with 2 teaspoons of filling and use a fork to seal the crust.

3 Insert into an Air fryer. At 390 degrees, cook for eight minutes until golden brown.

Chocolate Meringue Cookies

PREP TIME: 10 MINUTES • COOKING TIME: 60 MINUTES • TOTAL COOKING TIME: 1 HOUR 30 MINUTES • ***SERVES: 16 COOKIES***

Ingredients

¼ cup Swerve confectioners'-style sweetener
3 large egg whites
¼ teaspoon cream of tartar
2 tablespoons unsweetened cocoa powder

Direction:

1. Preheat the Salter air fryer to 225 °F. Line a 7-inch pie pan or dish compatible with an air fryer with parchment paper. In a separate dish, using a hand mixer, beat the egg whites and cream of tartar until soft peaks form. While the mixer is on low, sprinkle in the sweetener and mix until it is well combined. Continue to whip the mixture with an electric mixer until stiff peaks form. Add the cocoa powder and gently fold it in until incorporated. Place the mixture in a three-quarter-inch-tipped pastry bag. If you do not have a piping bag, create a 34-inch-wide hole in the corner of a big resealable plastic bag. Using a piping bag, sixteen 1-inch meringue cookies are piped onto the prepared pie pan at intervals of fourteen-twentieths of an inch.

2. Place the pan in the air fryer and cook for one hour, or until the exterior of the cookies is crisp. Turn off the air fryer after one hour and allow the cookies rest for twenty minutes before serving.

Lemon Poppy Seed Macaroons

PREP TIME: 10 MINUTES • COOKING TIME: 14 MINUTES • TOTAL COOKING TIME: 24 MINUTES • *SERVES: 12 COOKIES*

Ingredients

2 tablespoons grated lemon zest, plus more for garnish if desired
2 teaspoons poppy seeds
LEMON ICING:
¼ cup Swerve confectioners'-style sweetener
1 teaspoon lemon extract
¼ teaspoon fine sea salt
2 cups unsweetened shredded coconut
2 large egg whites, room temperature
⅓ cup Swerve confectioners'-style sweetener
1 tablespoon lemon juice

Direction:

1 Adjust the temperature of the Salter air fryer to 325 degrees Fahrenheit. Line an air fryer-compatible 7-inch pie plate or casserole dish with parchment paper. In a medium bowl, whisk the egg whites on high speed with a hand mixer until stiff peaks form. To the mixture, add the sugar, lemon zest, poppy seeds, lemon extract, and salt. Mix on low until completely combined. By incorporating the coconut with a rubber spatula. Place the cookies on the parchment paper using a one-inch cookie scoop, allowing about a quarter-inch between each one.

2 Cook for 12 to 14 minutes, or until a toothpick inserted into the center of the cookies emerges clean. Prepare the lemon icing while the cookies are in the oven: In a small basin, the sugar should be placed. Add lemon juice and fully combine. Add a touch extra sugar if the frosting is too thin. If the frosting is very thick, add more lemon juice. Remove the cookies from the air fryer and allow them to cool for approximately ten minutes prior to icing. Optional garnish consisting of lemon zest.

Blueberry Lemon Muffins

PREP TIME: 5 MINUTES • COOKING TIME: 10 MINUTES • TOTAL COOKING TIME: 15 MINUTES • *SERVES: 12*

Ingredients

1 tsp. vanilla
Juice and zest of 1 lemon
2 eggs
1 C. blueberries
½ C. cream

¼ C. avocado oil
½ C. monk fruit
2 ½ C. almond flour

Direction:

1. Combining flour with monk fruit.
2. Combine vanilla, egg, lemon juice, and cream in a separate bowl. Add mixtures and thoroughly blend them. Fill cupcake cases with batter.
3. Place within an air fryer. 10 minutes at 320 degrees Fahrenheit; check after 6 minutes to prevent overbaking.

Lemon Curd Pavlova

PREP TIME: 10 MINUTES •COOKING TIME: 60 MINUTES •TOTAL COOKING TIME: 1 HOUR 30 MINUTES • ***SERVES: 4***

Ingredients

¾ cup Swerve confectioners'-style sweetener
1 teaspoon grated lemon zest
1 teaspoon lemon extract
FOR GARNISH (OPTIONAL):
Blueberries
1 cup Swerve confectioners'-style sweetener or powdered sweetener
½ cup lemon juice
4 large eggs
½ cup coconut oil
3 large egg whites
¼ teaspoon cream of tartar
Swerve confectioners'-style sweetener or equivalent amount of powdered sweetener

Direction:

1. Bring the Salter air fryer to a temperature of 275 degrees Fahrenheit. Thoroughly grease a 7-inch pie dish with butter or coconut oil.
2. Construct the shell: In a separate dish, using a hand mixer, beat the egg whites and cream of tartar until soft peaks form. While the mixer is on low, sprinkle in the sweetener and mix until it is well combined.
3. After adding lemon zest and lemon extract, continue mixing with a hand mixer until stiff peaks form.
4. Spread the mixture evenly over the bottom, up the sides, and onto the rim of the pie pan to form the crust.
5. After one hour of cooking, switch off the air fryer and allow the shell to rest for twenty minutes. (If preferred, the shell can be prepared three days in advance and refrigerated in an airtight container.)
6. Prepare the lemon curd while the pastry is baking. In a medium saucepan with a heavy bottom, combine sugar, lemon juice, and eggs. Add the coconut oil and place the pan on the burner over medium heat. After the oil has melted, whisk the mixture constantly for

approximately 10 minutes, or until it has thickened and coated the back of a spoon. Do not allow the mixture to boil.

7 Pour the lemon curd mixture through a fine-mesh strainer into a medium basin. Place the bowl in a larger basin filled with ice water and whisk intermittently for 15 minutes, or until the curd has cooled completely.

8 Place the lemon curd on top of the crust, and if desired, sprinkle blueberries and powdered sugar on top. Refrigerate leftovers for up to four days.

CONCLUSION

We must consume food to live. As a result, food has come to represent affection, care, and community. Recording, collecting, sharing, and remembering the family recipes you have inherited is a wonderful way to immortalize and respect your family. These traditions are what shape your individuality. By cooking these recipes, you will not only be honoring your family heritage, but you will also be inspired to create your own modifications, which you may then pass on to your offspring. No one truly owns the recipes; they are simply shared with everyone. I enjoy sharing recipes as well. Numerous home cooks have contributed to the collection so that we can all prepare delectable dishes at home. I am grateful to everyone who has contributed to this book and allowed their traditions to be passed on to others and grow. You guys are fantastic!

RECIPES INDEX

ABOUT THE AUTHOR

Cynthia Blanchette is a freelance writer who focuses on cuisine, wine, and travel as areas of expertise. She has worked in the field of food and wine for over 15 years now and has a wealth of knowledge. She posts recipes, ideas for food and wine pairings, and food and wine travel guides on guest sites that she is a contributor to. She is a mother of three adolescents, and one of her goals is to create scrumptious, elevated, daily recipes and simple meal plans that any home cook can make in less time, with fewer ingredients, and a whole lot of love. She wants to share these with other home cooks so that they can pass on their own love of cooking to their children. Her intention is to make these available to other people who cook at home.

Printed in Great Britain
by Amazon

15285130R00072